Evaluation without Tears

Evaluation without Tears

101 Ways to Evaluate the Work of Students

Selma Wassermann

ROWMAN & LITTLEFIELD
Lanham • Boulder • New York • London

Published by Rowman & Littlefield
An imprint of The Rowman & Littlefield Publishing Group, Inc.
4501 Forbes Boulevard, Suite 200, Lanham, Maryland 20706
www.rowman.com

6 Tinworth Street, London SE11 5AL, United Kingdom

Copyright © 2020 by Selma Wassermann

All rights reserved. No part of this book may be reproduced in any form or by any electronic or mechanical means, including information storage and retrieval systems, without written permission from the publisher, except by a reviewer who may quote passages in a review.

British Library Cataloguing in Publication Information Available

Library of Congress Cataloging-in-Publication Data

Names: Wassermann, Selma, author.
Title: Evaluation without tears : 101 ways to evaluate the work
   of students / Selma Wassermann.
Description: Lanham : Rowman & Littlefield, [2020] | Includes bibliographical references and index. | Summary: "This tackles the fallacies of marking and grading students' work and provides teachers with specific examples of how they might provide evaluative feedback to students that enables and promotes their subsequent growth on learning tasks"— Provided by publisher.
Identifiers: LCCN 2019045068 (print) | LCCN 2019045069 (ebook) |
   ISBN 9781475853490 (cloth) | ISBN 9781475853506 (paperback) |
   ISBN 9781475853513 (epub)
Subjects: LCSH: Grading and marking (Students) | Teacher-student relationships. | Educational tests and measurements.
Classification: LCC LB3051 .W36 2020 (print) | LCC LB3051 (ebook) |
   DDC 371.27/2—dc23
LC record available at https://lccn.loc.gov/2019045068
LC ebook record available at https://lccn.loc.gov/2019045069

Contents

Preface	vii
Acknowledgments	xi
Introduction	xiii

1 What's Evaluation for? 1
    Force of Habit 1
    What's Evaluation for? 3

2 Marking and Grading: The Tail that Wags the Dog 7
    A House of Cards 10

3 A Case for Using Evaluative Feedback 17
    Evaluation as Feedback 19
    Obstacles to Using Evaluative Feedback in Lieu of Grades ... 20

4 Evaluative Feedback that Enables and Promotes Growth ... 23
    Checklist for Giving Evaluative Feedback 24
    Identifying the Criteria: What Are We Looking for? ... 25
    What Is Being Measured? 25
    Learning Goals and Evaluation Practices 26
    Goals for a Science Program 27

5 Written Diagnostic Evaluative Feedback across the Curriculum ... 29
    Examples from the Primary Grades Across the Curriculum ... 30
    Examples from the Intermediate Grades across the Curriculum ... 37
    Examples from the Secondary School across the Curriculum ... 43
    Conclusion 52

6	It's All About How You Say It	55
	Reflecting in Action	55
	Examining Classroom Discussions	57
	Hooked on Praise	64
7	Impediments to Good Diagnostic Judgment	67
	Taming the Impulse to Punish by Evaluative Judgment	69
	Two Cents Worth of Advice to Teachers	70
8	Reporting to Parents	73
	Examples of Written Reports to Parents	74
	Parent-Teacher and Parent-Student-Teacher Conferences	78
9	Students as Self-Evaluators	83
	Children Evaluating Themselves in the Primary Grades: The Child in the Process	86
	Written Self-Evaluation Reports in the Primary Grades	87
	Students Evaluating Themselves in a One-on-One Tutorial	89
	Students Evaluating Themselves in the Secondary School	91
	Teachers' Assessments on the Profiles	105
	Conclusion	106
10	Institutional Changes toward Using Evaluative Feedback in Reporting to Parents	107
	Examples of Schools that "Dare to be Different"	108
	Conclusion	117
11	Evaluation as a Subversive Activity: What Can a Teacher Do?	119
	End Note	122
12	Postscript: A Personal Odyssey	123
	A Professional Journey	123
Bibliography		127
Index		131
About the Author		135

Preface

When I was a child in elementary school, I believed, as most of us did in those days, that the marks and grades I received on homework assignments, test papers, and report cards defined me. The lessons implicit in marks and grades were that my worth was measured by those numbers and letters, and that if I got less than a high mark, I would be deemed inadequate. Alas, this was not only true of me. It was the *sine qua non* for every one of us, and in every grade.

These institutional building blocks were aided and abetted by my parents, who poured over my papers and report cards as if they were the Ten Commandments, handed down by God and given to my teacher to be passed out to her students. Unlike other children who were rewarded by money for good grades, or skiing trips to Aspen for a perfect score on a test, I received no parental prizes. The expectation was that I would get the good grades that would indicate to them that I was a "top" student and that I was not shirking my responsibilities to learn what was on offer in those classrooms. If I happened to get a grade of 98% on a test, my father would admonish me with "What happened to 100%?"

Marks and grades were the singular indicators not only of measures of performance, but of personal worth and value. Students who received less than good marks were considered "less"—and those of us in the upper echelon of the grading hierarchy were disinclined to associate with them. Not only did our grades define us; they defined those with whom we were wont to associate with. What was never an issue was the often unfairness of those numbers and letters, the arbitrary nature of what was being measured, and how those measurements were made.

Of course, grades did more than define us. It opened doors for us to higher education—since they were taken as indicators of whether we were not only eligible but deserving of a place in colleges and universities—making something more of ourselves than our left-behind classmates whose grades were the crushing signifiers of their lesser worth. Good grades entitled us; gave us a "can do" spirit. Poor grades disqualified others, giving them a "can't do" spirit. No one questioned the fairness of unfairness of any of it.

It wasn't until my first semester at college that this embedded notion that grades equaled a realistic assessment of capability and worth was shattered. In a freshman English class with two of my best friends, the three of us wet behind the ears and full of ourselves as having made it into the prestigious city university, we were given an assignment to write something—I can't remember what—by our distinguished professor, who looked as learned as a small owl with glasses. My two friends folded; neither of them felt up to the task of creating something on paper that was original, smart, and meeting the standards of college English. "Never mind," I told them, without a thought to the illegality or immorality of what I was proposing. I thought only of helping them.

So I sat down to write three papers for Professor Stair, and my two friends and I handed in each, under their and my names.

When the papers were returned, both friends got As. My paper not only got a C—but was marked in red comments that crushed me: I was not a good writer. How did I ever manage to get into college? There was no chance I would pass this course unless I improved considerably.

Once over the shock of these diminishing blows to my self-esteem, I began to see the frailty of the marking and grading system and how fallible one teacher's assessments can be. I was finally able to shed the deeply entrenched idea that marks and grades were truths about self and performance, but only one person's judgment, which is not truth, but opinion. And as many of us know, opinions are shaped and formed by many factors, some of which are spurious, some of which are mean-spirited, and some of which are larded with *schadenfreude*.

Yet, there's another side to the coin of marking and grading—and that is the side referred to as "evaluation." For while evaluation may include the assigning of marks and grades, it is also the case that evaluative comments on students' papers and on student performance can enable and empower a student to do better, to improve, and to make additional gains in understanding and in levels of performance. Evaluation, of course, can be as cruel and as punishing as Professor Stair's comments on that English paper. But in the hands of a wise, informed, and skillful teacher, evaluative comments can be more than additive.

It is the purpose of this book to shed light on the history of how marks and grades came to signify student worth, what factors lie beneath a teacher's assessments, the fallibility of marks and grades as signifiers of intelligence, the reliance we put on grades as truth, why teachers should instead use written comments as feedback instead of numbers and letters, and, most important, how to give evaluative feedback to students that does not diminish them but actually provides them with the means and the support to deepen their understanding and improve their skills in subsequent tasks.

It is not an easy task—since the history of marks and grades are so woven into the educational process and into our culture that we have come to consider them as set in stone. But anyone who has felt the sting of an evaluation that has been unfair, unwise, and just plain wrong will want to consider the imperative of a changed approach to student assessment that is more honest, fair, and, especially, more helpful to student growth and learning. How can that be a task not worth tackling?

Acknowledgments

No book is the work of a single person and there is a large group of people to whom I am indebted for their contributions that added immeasurably to the writing of this book. Teacher-colleagues that I called on to provide samples of students' work that informed the way teachers give evaluative feedback at the elementary and secondary school levels were more than generous in their responses. Steve Fukui, teacher, colleague, and friend sent me samples of his students' work from his social studies and law classes at Terry Fox Senior Secondary School in Coquitlam. Tami McDiarmid provided me with samples of her Grade 3-4 students' work from Charles Dickens Elementary School in Vancouver. Maya Snow and Kai Snow graciously allowed me to use their writings and drawings; Simon Snow, the wizard of Parksville, always on call for help with IT issues and photos makes my writing life that much easier. George Sturm sent samples of his son Max's work from Dwight-Englewood Elementary School. All of these rich examples of student work gave me the primary data to use to show how evaluative feedback can be used in enabling and productive ways.

Colleagues from near and far afield were generous in offering to read and review the manuscript and I thank them for their feedback and their wisdom: Dr. Larry Cuban, Ms. Annie O'Donaghue, Dr. Katie McAllister, Dr. Bill C. Cliett, Jr., and Dr. Maurice Gibbons. Your words of affirmation for this new work fill me with gratitude.

Richard Dancy, Reference Archivist at Simon Fraser University, went to great lengths to search the Wassermann archives and locate articles that I needed to support my arguments.

And for their permission to use material from previously published articles:

Anne Bauer, Editor. Association for Childhood Education International for "What's Evaluation For?" Winter, 1991, pp. 93–96;

Teachers College Press, for the use of transcripts "Garbage," and "Locusts" and the Goal Statements, from Selma Wassermann and J. W. George Ivany, *The New Teaching Elementary Science: Who's Afraid of Spiders?* 2nd edition, Teachers College Press. Copyright 1996, by Teachers College, Columbia University. All rights reserved. And for the materials about parent-teacher-child conferences and self-evaluation, from Selma Wassermann, *Serious Players in the Primary Classroom: Empowering Children Through Active Learning Experiences*, 2nd edition. New York: Teachers College Press. Copyright 2000 by Teachers College, Columbia University. All rights reserved.

And, finally, to my publisher, Tom Koerner, for his faith and confidence in my work.

My heartfelt thanks to you all.

Introduction

Anyone who has spent any time with a teacher, whether in school, in a tutorial, or with a mentor, or coach has felt the slings and arrows of evaluative feedback. Anyone who has put his or her creation or performance out to public view has experienced affirmation or castigation from self-appointed critics. Anyone who has grown up in a household with well-meaning parents has heard or felt acclaim or discouragement as part of their growth and development. In short, evaluative utterances are a constant in one's life, whether we are students, teachers, performers, artists, or just ordinary citizens walking the paths of life.

In the best of circumstances, evaluation is a process that should provide feedback to learners that enables their subsequent growth. When it is enabling, it is affirming, rather than punishing, respectful of the learner, and protective of a learner's dignity. It is also specific in what the criteria for judgment are, and clear in how the work meets or fails to meet the standards.

When evaluative feedback is helpful, it enables a learner to make the next steps in the learning process and opens doors to greater understanding and skill development.

There are times when evaluative feedback, rather than enables, disables. And when that feedback is hurtful, delivered sometimes with well-meaning intentions, it can handicap a learner for a lifetime:

"Robert, you are the least talented music student I have ever met."

"Your story makes no sense to me. Obviously, you haven't worked very hard at it."

"Your spelling is atrocious. Use the dictionary!"

"Eight examples wrong out of ten? You aren't thinking!"

"If you don't pull up your socks, you'll never amount to anything in life."

There are groups of people whose job is to give evaluative feedback in specific performance areas, like music, art, theater, literature, and sports, and who are the supposed well-informed assessors of competence, worth, and value:

"Beethoven always sounds to me like the upsetting of bags of nails, with here and there an also dropped hammer" (Slonimsky, 1965).

"History of a Soldier is a degenerate and eviscerated product of the composer, music written without enthusiasm, certainly without faith and without pity" (Downes, 1928).

"An American in Paris (Gershwin) is nauseous claptrap, so dull, patchy, thin, vulgar, long-winded and inane, that the average movie audience would be bored by it" (Peyser, 1928).

"Pablo Picasso's work is schizophrenic and satanic; it is an underworld form, something that is evil and does not belong in art galleries."

"Van Gogh's work is amateurish, strange intense and feverish."

J. K. Rowling is reported to have had seventeen rejections for her first Harry Potter manuscript before she found a publisher who was willing to take a risk and publish it.

The truth of evaluative comments is that they are not truths. They come from the personal perspectives of the evaluators, opinions that lie in the eyes of the beholders. What they rest on are not only personal values and personal ideas of what is good but also an evaluator's sense of what meets current cultural and ethical standards.

The original judgments about Beethoven, Van Gogh, Gershwin, Picasso, to name a few whose work was originally condemned, has now been completely reversed: Van Gogh's painting of Portrait of Dr. Gachet sold, at auction, for a record $82.5 million; Beethoven is considered one of the greatest of all classical composers; Stravinsky is thought of as one of the most important and influential composers of the twentieth century; *An American in Paris* won an Academy Award and is regarded as one of the best American musicals; Picasso's painting, Nude, Green Leaves and Bust, sold for $106.5 million in 2010. J. K. Rowling has sold more than 500 *million* copies worldwide of her Harry Potter books. And of course, James Joyce's *Ulysses*, thought to be "obscene" and banned from publication in 1933, is now considered a masterwork.

Another side of the coin vis-à-vis evaluating students' work is the assigning of marks and grades. To be clear, evaluation is based on some articulated or unspecified set of standards and comes in the form of written statements. Marks and grades, on the other hand, are administrative conveniences that come in the form of letters and numbers. They represent a quantification of where a student "ranks" in relationship to others and measured against subject norms. Evaluative comments may lead to a grade; however, grades may stand on their own, without any written evaluative feedback. More often than not, they are issued on the basis of what is considered "right" and "wrong" in a student's work.

Despite its long history in education practice, and despite the considerable reliance on grades as indicators of students' academic standing and measures of academic worth, grading has very bad marks (forgive the pun) as reliable measures. Going back to the early twentieth century, Finklestein (1913) noted, "When we consider the practically universal use in all educational institutions of a system of marks, whether numbers or letters, to indicate scholastic attainment of the pupils or students in these institutions, and when we remember how very great stress is laid by teachers and pupils alike upon these marks as real measures or indicators of attainment, we can be but astonished at the blind faith that has been felt in the reliability of the marking system. School administrators have been using with confidence an absolutely uncalibrated instrument."

"Variability in the marks given for the same subject and to the same pupils by different instructors is so great as frequently to work real injustice to the students . . . nor may anyone seek refuge in the assertion that the marks of the students are of little real importance. The evidence is clear that marks constitute a very real and a very strong inducement to work, that they are accepted as real and fairly exact measurements of ability or of performance. Moreover, they not infrequently are determiners of the student's career" (Finkelstein, 1913).

Yet, marks and grades endure as indicators of what's right and what's wrong in students' work. And today, more than 100 years later, marks and grades are more than ever the determining factors in a student's future.

Given all of the above—the errors, the inconsistencies, the frailties of human judgment—should one abandon altogether evaluative feedback and marks and grades, especially as they have been shown to be specious, less than helpful, and sometimes more harmful to student growth? Or, are there better ways of evaluating a student's work so that he or she is enabled by the feedback and helped in understanding the big ideas and in advancing his or her skills on particular tasks?

It is the purpose of this text not only to point out the frailties of the marking, grading, and evaluation systems in schools but also to examine the history of how marks and grades became the *sine qua non* of school learning, what factors lie beneath a teacher's assessments, the reliance we put on grades as true measures of a student's worth, why teachers and administrators rely on marks and grades, and, most important, how to give evaluative feedback to students that does not diminish them, but actually provides them with the means and the support to deepen their understanding and improve their skills.

The book is organized in twelve chapters. The first four provide an overview of how we became obsessed with marks and grades, the history of how marks and grades came into being in schools as well as their validity and reliability, how marks and grades are used as indicators of student learning, and the nature of evaluative comments found on student papers. Chapters 5, 6, and 7 provide a rationale for using enabling evaluative feedback and offer numerous examples of how this is done in several curriculum areas. Chapter 8 offers suggestions for ways of reporting to parents in both written and conference forms with the additional factor of including students in parent-teacher conferences.

Chapter 9 offers a rationale for involving students in self-assessments. Chapter 10 highlights different schools' shifting of gears in abandoning letter and number grades in favor of anecdotal and narrative reports. Chapter 11 offers suggestions for teachers who are constrained by reporting systems that rely on number and letter grades. Finally, in a postscript, the author discloses her own journey from marking and grading to more student-centered strategies.

Chapter 1

What's Evaluation for?

Pat O'Donnell, the curriculum supervisor for Marin County, related a story of his wife, who, at Easter time, would buy a large ham to cook for the Easter Sunday family gathering. He would watch her chop off the end of the ham and discard it before putting it into the roasting pan, and she did this each Easter, without fail. When Pat asked her why she cut off the end of the ham and discarded it, she said, "My mother always did it that way."

On a visit to his mother-in-law's house the following week, Pat asked her the reason for cutting off the ends of hams before roasting. She answered, "My mother always did it that way."

When Pat got around to visiting Grandmother Morgan's home, he was determined to get at the root of the puzzle and asked her about why she cut off the ends of her ham before roasting. She told him, "Because my pan is too small."

As John Dewey reminded us, "We grow to love our chains."

FORCE OF HABIT

Our habits stick to us like glue. We get stuck on eating oatmeal for breakfast each morning and pancakes only on Sundays. We become habituated to reading the *New York Times* and disdain any other newspaper as not worth our time. We can't seem to take a walk, or ride a bicycle, or go to the market without our cell phones in our hands, checking obsessively to see who is trying to reach us by text or e-mail. We can't conclude the day without tuning in to the late news. Rituals become embedded in our psyches; they become a part of us, of who we are, and how we interact with the world.

Although habits differ with each individual, there is one defining feature to all of them. They are done without thought. We carry out our habits without a second glance at why we are doing that or what the implications are of our behavior. They are habits.

Our ordinary habits are not in the same league as those rituals of the obsessive person. With obsessive compulsive disorder (OCD), the sufferer *must* behave in certain ways, carry out certain moves, with the underlying and implicit reason that such behaviors protect him or her. Our non-OCD habits are initially chosen. And although they have become ingrained within us, to lose them is not life threatening. Giving them up may make us uncomfortable, or moody; but having eggs and toast in lieu of oatmeal may neither shake us to our roots nor cause the sky to fall.

The heavy reliance on marks and grades in the public schools has become a deep-rooted, persistent, and pernicious habit. And like the women who persisted in lopping off the end of the ham before cooking, the entire educational system, one generation after the other, has embraced them, to the extent that they have become the be all and end all of what school and learning is all about. Never mind the fact that there is a large and persuasive body of literature that points to the errors, the fallacies, the problems, and the inaccuracies of marks and grades.

The consequence of this is that there exists a huge disconnect between what evaluation is for—what it is supposed to do in diagnosing problems and enabling further learning—and the issuing of numbers and letters on a student's work. Imagine building such a tower of conviction on such shaky grounds, for as Finkelstein wrote more than hundred years ago, "School administrators have been using with confidence an absolutely uncalibrated instrument" (Finkelstein, 1913), instruments that are notoriously unreliable and inaccurate (Combs, 1979). The end result is that we are lopping off the end of the ham just because our school system has always done it that way. It is a nonthinking approach to evaluation, a habit deeply engrained in what we do in schools.

Attempts at changing such ingrown habits are frustrated by the "grammar of schooling," a term coined by Tyack and Cuban (1995) to describe how the infrastructure of school organizations are so cemented in place that any endeavor to make radical and innovative shifts in practice, no matter how relevant or reasonable, have few chances to survive, let alone take root. Like water seeking its own level, changes appear and then vanish. And old habits resume their inbred positions.

One consequence of all of this is that students have come to believe that the marks and grades they receive are not only indicators of their worth but define them and their future not only in the academic world, but beyond. Good marks are green lights to a theoretically more successful and productive life. Poor marks are more than just marks. They carry heavy weight; in too many cases, they are impediments to future success and healthful growth and development. Is it any wonder that students "angle" for As no matter at what price? Grades have long displaced learning as the important goal of education. "If I don't need to know it for the test, then I don't need to know it."

Another abuse of marking and grading is the way that teachers, especially for sports events, reward children equally for what they have done. "Everyone gets a star," no matter how well or poorly he or she has performed. In an attempt to "even the playing field," this exercise of giving out rewards for excellence is prostituted. No one is fooled, especially the children. The child who brings home a "star" even though he or she knows that he or she has performed poorly has participated in a lie—and that's a harsh reality to take home.

Gaming the system has now become entrenched as students have learned to outfox the ways in which grades are assigned, making final grades more specious than ever. And why should we be surprised to learn that parents have used various ruses and swindles to obtain places in prestigious colleges and universities for their "entitled" but poorly graded offspring?

Yes, the ingrained habits of marking and grading have definite downsides. For some students, it takes years after school to learn that their grades and marks do not define them and their potential. But others never get that insight and they remain trapped in a cowl of feelings of low worth.

The history of how marks and grades took such firm hold in education will be addressed in the next chapter—a history of how these habits, with spurious rationale, became embedded in our culture. But before that, it may be essential to address the "big ideas" of evaluation. That is, what is it for? And how do we connect what we actually do with the reasons for doing it?

WHAT'S EVALUATION FOR?

No one questions the need for evaluating students' work as they progress from grade to grade in school settings. No one questions the importance of using evaluation as a tool to guide students to improve their work, to increase their understanding, to show them the ways, and the means to gain a foothold on the next step of the ladder of learning.

The administrative convenience that has contributed to the use of grades and marks as indicators of how much a student has learned and where that student "ranks" among members of his or her class has allowed educators to neglect the important principles on which evaluative practices rest. When these principles are ignored or subverted, evaluation becomes a meaningless or, worse, a punitive system. When the principles are allowed to inform practice, evaluation becomes an important process for enhancing student learning.

First, evaluation is a process that provides feedback to learners that enables subsequent growth. This feedback may be helpful or hurtful. It may enable or disable. If evaluation is to be enabling, it should be affirming, rather than punishing, respectful of the student and protective of that student's dignity. Above all, it must be honest.

Yes, we educators can find ways to indicate to a student what needs another look, what needs correction, what is in error, where the data should be supported by documentation—and the ways to do this are not in the sleight of hand. It's a matter of how one phrases the evaluative comments. Chapters 5 and 6 are explicit in showing how this is done.

Second, an important goal of evaluation is to shift the locus of evaluation from teachers to learners, so that learners become more informed self-evaluators. Although this is a rarely seen occurrence in public education, the *raison d'etre* of it is to provide students with the tools to become their own diagnosticians, liberating them to take the steps that allow for ongoing, lifelong learning outside the classroom. When teachers guard their right to keep the locus of evaluation for themselves, they deny students the opportunity for lifelong, independent learning and students will always look to others to determine if their work is "good."

Several procedures enable this process:

- The teacher makes judgments personal to the evaluator, rather than issuing them as authoritative truths.
- The teacher, as a rule, requires students to make their own diagnostic assessments of their own work based upon clearly identified criteria.
- The teacher provides students with self-evaluative tools that they may use in promoting their growth in self-assessment.
- The teacher accepts students' self-evaluations without assuming the role of final judge of whether or not the self-evaluation is "correct."

More about student self-evaluation is found in chapter 9.

Third, evaluation requires the ability to diagnose weaknesses and strengths in a learner's performance. This is based on the articulation of specific criteria that are explicit or implicit requirements of the learning task. Diagnosis goes beyond the simple determination of value (good/bad/right/wrong) to illustrate how the work meets or fails to meet the criteria. A teacher's diagnosis points to what the student needs to do to improve his or her subsequent learning. Diagnostic evaluation is the means through which feedback on a student's work is given. It is the basis for informed feedback to the student. In giving diagnostic feedback, it is helpful to

- be clear about the criteria used to make the judgments;
- make the criteria clear to the student;
- use the criteria to write clear and specific comments to the learner that point out how different aspects of the work meet or fail to meet the criteria;
- suggest ways in which the learner might take the next steps to improve his or her work on the task, making those suggestions specific;
- be selective in zeroing in on what is more important, rather than overwhelming the learner by attempting to deal with every aspect of the work that requires improvement; and
- remember that the feedback you give is your own notion of what's good and what needs improvement; it is not truth.

Fourth, the evaluative process enables teachers to give parents informed and helpful feedback about their children's work in school. Feedback to parents, like feedback to students, is more helpful when it is

- affirming, rather than punitive;
- respectful of the student and protective of the student's dignity;
- clear in how the work meets/fails to meet the criteria;
- specific in what the criteria for judging the work are;
- clear and free from jargon;
- concise and not excessively verbose;
- selective, and not overwhelming in attempting to deal with every aspect of the learner's performance;
- honest, fair, and genuine in teachers' comments to parents, recognizing their desires to see their own children as unfailingly wonderful; and
- empathic in being responsive to parents' concerns.

Fifth, thoughtful, careful, and relevant evaluation of student work is a higher-order thinking task on the teacher's part. It is hard to do, because it requires a great deal of reflection, much clarity about criteria and standards, thoughtful analysis and mental processing, and high-level professional skills in making appropriate responses. Like other higher-order mental functions, there are no right answers in evaluation, no shortcuts to the mental processing involved to do the job. Since evaluative judgments lie in the eye of the beholder, each evaluator brings his or her own values to bear on each judgment. As a consequence, the illusion that evaluation can be objective is only that: an illusion. This further complicates an already-complex process.

One improves one's skill as an evaluator with experience in the process and by subjecting one's evaluative work to critical self-scrutiny in relationship to the principles of evaluation. The ability to be critically aware and nondefensive in examining one's own evaluative strategies is key to the development of skill as an evaluator.

There is also the matter of how personal bias inevitably creeps into one's assessments. Being aware of one's own preferences and prejudices, and especially how they influence the evaluative judgments one makes, is one key to ensuring that those biases are kept in check and not allowed to infiltrate the feedback.

Sixth, it is important to remember, as mentioned above, that evaluation and grading are two different (and often unrelated) procedures. They have different purposes and different consequences. The process of evaluation is to diagnose, according to explicit and implicit criteria, and to provide feedback that informs subsequent learning. The purpose of grading is to assign a quantitative value to performance and to rank that performance in a hierarchical order. Ranking does not shift the locus of evaluation to the student, but rather maintains that locus in the teacher's domain.

In the final analysis, a teacher's beliefs about learning and about students will be the basis of the evaluative strategies he or she will use to assess student learning. To use evaluative feedback based on clearly articulated criteria, teachers must truly and deeply believe in evaluation that is enabling and affirming and in the importance of self-evaluation as a primary goal of education. Otherwise, the use of more effective and enabling evaluation strategies will once more, like other good ideas in education, pass into that good night.[1]

Explicit help in performing all of these functions is what this book is about—to focus attention on what is important to us in education, so that the ways of assessment are congruent with our overall educational goals.

NOTE

1. The section "What's Evaluation for?" has been extracted, with permission, from Selma Wassermann, "Teaching Strategies: What's Evaluation For?" in *Childhood Education*, Winter, 1991, pp. 93–98).

Chapter 2

Marking and Grading
The Tail that Wags the Dog

Some days you just can't do it.

— The legendary pianist Vladimir Horowitz, being interviewed about his extraordinary musical ability. David Dubal, 2004

Marilyn French's compelling but largely overlooked text *Beyond Power* (1985) provides one glimpse into the early history of how marks and grades came into being in public education and it is not a comforting picture. According to French, these rating systems came into existence as a result of attempts to rule and control the rising masses of immigrants who were descending, ship by ship, into the ports of the United States, seeking better lives in the early days of the nineteenth century. Many of those coming from veins of poverty were illiterate, impoverished, ragged. All of them were searching for more opportunities, more options to earn a living that would support them and their families.

To some, the arrival of masses of immigrants meant a good supply of cheap labor, much needed in the burgeoning new industrial age. Others, opposed to any newcomers, saw them as intruders—uncultured, unwashed, unwelcome, who represented a population that needed careful watching and careful control. It must be recalled that the "nineteenth century was a period of explosive violence in the United States, as labor fought for unionization, mobs rioted in economic despair, and groups fought each other in spasms of ethnic or religious hostility" (French, 1985).

Those explosions of violence were terrifying for those in power—those pockets of influence who saw the establishment threatened and who moved quickly to rein in the unruly masses who wanted nothing more than better working conditions, better wages, better housing, more equitable distribution of resources. Public education seemed the right and best way of exercising that control—a means of quelling the middle class's fears of mobs, immigration, socialism, and anarchy.

Those advocating for public schooling claimed that schools would remove the young from "corrupt homes and neighborhoods, and teach them order, regularity, industry, and temperance. Above all, they would be taught to obey and respect authority" (French, 1985).

"To persuade business of the advantages of education, its potential for curbing social unrest and an insurance policy against Bolshevism, sedition and any attempt to tear down the government, the schoolmen increasingly spoke in the language of the corporation. They argued that public education was the most humane form of *social control* and the safest method of social renewal" (French, 1985). Public education would train the next generation of workers in temperance, industry, and *obedience* to the bells and buzzers that divided the day in coercive institutions (italics by the author).

So public education, the demand for free schools, was built on the thesis that schools would be controlling forces to stem the tide of potential radical behaviors and keep the positions and powers of the middle and upper classes in control. To that end, the schools would be built on standardization and centralization of control, to serve to eliminate cultural distinctions, and to indoctrinate all children into "aggressive Protestantism, temperance, and English language chauvinism" (Tyack, 1974).

While, on the one hand, the initiative for creating public schools seemed humanitarian, progressive and democratic, it was, in its secret underbelly, racist. The new systems would exercise social control over the young, ensuring that they would never be a threat to the corporate powers. The schools were expected to produce workers who would take their place in a class of obedient toilers in a hierarchically structured labor force (Ryan, 1981; Bowles and Gintis, 1976).

To fulfill those shameful objectives, the educational system was built on corporate lines, with centralized control administered through a bureaucracy, the better way to keep not only students in check but to ensure that teachers followed the narrowly proscribed curriculum. Students who were supposed to be served by the system were treated as objects to be manipulated with disregard for their own needs and desires (French, 1985). A principal in New York when asked whether students were allowed to move their heads answered: "Why should they look behind them when the teacher is in front of them?" (Cremin, 1961).

Teachers were and still are, in many locales, to conform to a uniform curriculum, and had, and still have, little authorized autonomy. Curriculum and teaching methods could be regulated by local school boards that were made up primarily of business and professional men.

Not only students but also teachers were required to conform obediently and prevented from exercising any autonomy in their curricula or methods. The exercise of independent thought, by teachers or students, was strictly anathema. "Except in areas like mathematics and science, in which thinking is abstract, students were not encouraged to think at all" (French, 1985). A policy of racism pervaded public education and even today, despite strong initiatives for change, such inequities continue to exist in public school systems across the country.

It was in 1916 that the Stanford-Binet I.Q. test was introduced in schools, an instrument responsible for maintaining racist policies in education. Children were grouped on the basis of their test scores, and segregation by "intellectual levels" was nearly universally practiced. Of course, all this was done with the high moral sounding of "what were the best instructional practices." When test results were not congruent with expectations, the test questions were altered; questions that would show results not in keeping with expectations were removed (French, 1985).

This was the beginning of quantification in schools, and although schools no longer administer I.Q. tests, other forms of tests and quantification have replaced them, the basis of which was, and continues to be, the insidious goal of separating out the "betters" from the "less good," the pseudoscientific means of enabling institutions to label people as inferior, without the appearance of prejudice (French. 1985).

Standardized tests aided and abetted by federal initiatives like "No Child Left Behind," and "Common Core State Standards," became one more educational defining point for learners and big business for the test makers. The so-called non-profit Educational Testing Service reported a net income of $43,000,000 in 2016. The pressures then and now on teachers to measure and rank, rather than using evaluation to help students further their learning, has been a constant in educational practice for more than a hundred years.

Student performance on tests fix their positions in the learning hierarchy, positions that are more than likely to be immutable throughout their educational careers and afterward. Because of this, learning that awakens knowledge and deepens understanding has been trumped by the urgency of obtaining better marks. It is not an exaggeration to say that is true for every level of education, from the first years of school through the university.

Reform movements to change for the better and replace systems that are no longer educationally defensible have a dismal history of failure (Cuban, 1990). According to Tyack and Cuban (1995), this is largely a result of the organizational operations of schools, a system so ingrained in the institutional functions that they form a "grammar of schooling," a term coined by Tyack and Cuban to characterize the long-lasting and unchanging core elements of schooling.

And although teachers may close their doors, allowing them a few degrees of autonomy to make their own choices, the organizational system makes it difficult, if not impossible, for major change to take root and be sustained.

A HOUSE OF CARDS

Not only has measurement using grades and marks preempted the importance of learning to acquire knowledge and understanding, but it has other downsides as well. The system we have become locked into has erupted in a cascade of negative consequences about which educators, parents, and children know but are trapped by the system into helplessness.

First, and uppermost in the consideration of grades and marks is the singular unsoundness of the measures themselves. Again and again, the errors, inaccuracies, unreliability, and unfairness of these measurements have been decried, but the system persists, nevertheless. While they are accepted as real and exact measurements of ability or performance, they are, in fact, so spurious as to carry little weight as to their reliability and validity. This is true as much for teacher-assigned marks and grades, as they are for scores on standardized tests. There are numerous examples that confirm this, but, once again, it is a case of "don't confuse us with the data; our minds are made up."

For example, in order to test the hypothesis of variability in teachers' judgments of students' work, a first-year university student's English essay was submitted to five professors of English at a well-known university. The teachers were asked to "grade" the paper on a scale of 1 to 10, with 10 being the highest mark. None of the teachers graded the paper with the same score. The range of marks ranged from 4 to 10. Each teacher saw the student's paper through a different but highly personal lens of "what's good."

In another "test" for reliability, a third-grade student's arithmetic test paper was submitted to five elementary school teachers who were asked to grade the paper on a scale of 1 to 10. The belief was that when it came to assessing a student's work with algorithms, there would be little or no variability in the mark. In this case, too, the student's paper received a range of grades from 4 to 9. The teachers' marks revealed what each considered important in rating the student's work. There was no agreement among the teachers about the "true" mark.

One would think that in the case of a student's performance where single correct answers were clear and unambiguous, there would not be differences in grading, but this was not the case. Where grades are based on more tenuous performance levels, like written essays, the variability in marks and grades by even experienced teachers can be wide.

Not only do marks and grades lie in a teacher's perceptions of "what is good" but they also depend, in not small ways, on a teacher's state of mind while reading and marking. Ask any student about their teachers and they will tell you: "He's a hard marker." Or, "You should take Mrs. Jones for English. She's an easy marker." What does that say about the accuracy and validity of marks?

If one expected reliability and validity in testing on standardized tests, another example is offered to show the potential for error. In a grade 1 classroom, a designated day and time in the spring of the school year was set for the administration of a scholastic achievement test. Never mind the inappropriateness of using such an exam for grade 1. However, the decision was made by the school board, none of whom had any experience with first graders. As many first-grade teachers will recognize, most six-year-olds, in the spring of the school year, will be on the cusp of finding their ways in decoding the written word. Others will still be "emerging readers." This is the norm.

The students revealed their anxiety when the seating arrangements had to be changed to accommodate the "rules" issued by the test makers. The principal delivered the tests promptly at 9:45 a.m. and according to specific instructions, the tests were passed out to each child at exactly 10:00 a.m. All of these admonitions and specifications were to be followed scrupulously, as if the sky would fall if one varied from the regimen. At 10:15, the students opened the exam books and began to write.

Judy, aged 6, who seemed to skate through learning tasks as if each one had wheels, picked up her pencil and without a thought filled in the blanks, and proceeded in that fashion to the end of the section, as if the exam paper was a coloring-by-numbers book. Jimmy, a thoughtful, deliberate new reader, read each question as if trekking up Everest, and proceeded to complete seven examples correctly. Judy defied statistics, to achieve a score of 17 correct out of 30. Jimmy scored seven out of seven correctly.

A second failing of the marking and grading system is our "love affair" with numbers. Many of us have fallen into the trap of believing that a number represents truth. We tend to believe that within the numbers we see on report cards, on students' GPA's, on the thermometer hanging outside the door, on the blood pressure reading, on the numbers of votes cast for a candidate, on student ratings for their teachers, on the reading of the bathroom scale, lies certainty. And especially in times of turbulence in society, there is a tendency to cling to numbers to give us a sense of stability.

Today, we measure everything—time, distance, speed, size, weight, temperature, even the windchill factor so we can know how cold we should feel.

We measure angles, curves, and spatial relationships. Global positioning systems allow us to measure where we are in space.

We can now be assured that a 6.5 ounce can of tuna contains 106 calories, 24 grams of protein, and 1.1 grams of fat (of which 0.4 are polyunsaturated fats, 0.2 monosaturated fats, 0.2 saturated fats), 30 mg. of cholesterol, and 0 grams of carbohydrates per 100 gram serving. What's more, with the use of statistics and probability, we measure things that we cannot even see: the likelihood that the stock market will recover during this fiscal year, the chances for rain during the coming year in the Midwest, the numbers of salmon anticipated in the spring run, the force of a hurricane, the rate of global warming, the risk involved in a certain investment.

Our obsession with numbers has led us into the deep waters of quantification, and we now have rating scales for nearly everything, relying on these measures to guide our life choices. Zagat's tells us which restaurants receive ratings that make our dining there worthwhile; Ebert and Siskel invented the "thumbs up" sign for their approval of a new film; now the Internet provides us with ratings of hotels, restaurants, films and airlines, among others. "Rate your doctor" and "rate your professor" sites abound on the Internet, so that anyone can "weigh in" with a score. Woe be to the naif who takes such evaluations seriously.

The Dodecahedron of *The Phantom Tollbooth* describes our love affair with numbers: "If you had high hopes how would you know how high they were. And did you know that narrow escapes come in all different widths? Would you travel the whole wide world without ever knowing how wide it was? And how could you do anything at long last without knowing how long the last was? Why numbers are the most beautiful and valuable things in the world" (Juster, 1961).

Yet, the more we strive for accuracy in our numerical ratings, the more it eludes us. Take, for example, the measurement of time, in which nanosecond precision matters for worldwide communications systems and calculations must be constantly adjusted to accommodate for the anomalies in astronomical reference points. "It is the heavens that cannot be relied on. Stars drift. The earth shivers ever so slightly. With the oceanic tides acting as brakes, the planet slows in its rotation by fractions of a second each year. To compensate, the official clocks must every so often perform a grudging two-step, adding an odd second—a leap second—to the world's calendar" (Gleick, 1999).

At the Directorate of Time, Gernot M. R. Winkler, whose position requires the keeping of exact time by worldwide consensus and decree, says, "A Man with a watch knows what time it is. A man with two watches is never sure" (Gleick, 1999).

It is, however, a false sense of security that numbers bring. For when we eschew reality and accept numbers in the place of what we know, we are in great danger of self-delusion. Thus, when a student brings home a report card with a B, or a 98 percent in social studies, we would do well to look behind the number and find out what it is the student actually knows and if that is actually worth knowing. The number or letter means nothing.

A third, and perhaps most insidious failing is a student's belief that the letter or number he or she receives on a report card, or a test, or an assignment, is an actual representation of that student's worth. Give a student a repeated series of poor marks, and the unhappy result is that he or she will learn that he or she is "less," or, worse, "dumb." Once that die has been cast, it is difficult, perhaps impossible, for a student to break out of that trap of feeling incompetent. The system is self-perpetuating; more low marks contribute more to a sense of inadequacy; more feelings of inadequacy lead to more low marks. No teacher sets out to harm students; but the marking and grading system does that for him or her. Never mind what such a number or score means about what the student has learned.

Fourth, the system of letters and grades to signify a student's competence has now become the gateway to higher education. Despite the unreliability of those numbers and letters, many college and university admissions continue to hold them as keys to student acceptance. Is it any wonder that students have learned to "game the system" and that parents have found illegal ways to secure positions for their entitled children in prestigious universities, thus defeating the very purpose of the marks themselves? Is it any wonder that students have learned to value the mark or grade over what is important to learn in a course? "Is this going to be on the exam?" means "I don't have to learn it if it is not going to count toward my mark."

There is some irony in that the system we have adhered to in the educational process has subverted the process of education itself. As Derek Bok has written, "There is some fear that once a process of assessment takes hold, colleges will become preoccupied with those forms of learning that can be measured and neglect the subtler yet equally important educational goals that do not lend themselves to testing and evaluation" (Bok, 2006). Or, as Wilhelms and Diederich wrote, "The traditional system of marking and grading and credit granting is so inadequate and distorting, such a nuisance to good teaching and learning, that we simply have to throw it out and get ourselves something better" (Wilhelms and Diederich, 1967).

Fifth is the matter of how we perceive a student's performance as a constant—that is, no matter the weather, nor the time of day, the physical condition of the student, or whatever stresses or troubles he or she brings from home, nor any number of other factors, any person's performance at a particular task or job or activity is variable. As Horowitz, the legendary concert pianist told his interviewer, "Some days you can't do it."

Any one of us has had experiences in which we can perform a task well and are delighted with the results. And then there are days when, howsoever we approach the same task, we seem to get stuck, or perform badly. This is true whether you are plunking in letters on the keyboard of your computer, or playing a Bach Cello Suite, or trying to write a paragraph for a short story. Some days you just can't do it.

But in schools, we expect students to perform, on demand, at their best, despite other conditions that may prevail in their lives. And we expect their performance to be constant, never varying, never having a bad day. How then to judge or assess them fairly?

A sixth failing involves the "what" of grading and marking—that is, what actually is being measured in assessing students' work?

Most classroom assignments and tests are teacher made. In some instances, they ask for the most arcane pieces of information to "test" whether students have remembered what was lodged in the second to last paragraph on page 143 of the geography text. In some instances, they ask for calculation; for the names and dates of the explorers; for the three causes of World War I; for matching up the names of plays with their authors; for definitions of new vocabulary words.

A brief examination of a large quantity of teacher-made tests reveals that most of them, if not all, ask for simple answers to complex questions. Many of the questions, to our shame, ask for information that is irrelevant, or plain wrong. Students are expected to give the teacher the "right" answer that the teacher had in his or her mind.

In what year did Shakespeare graduate from high school?
What were the three causes of World War I?
What are the three human races?

Yet, these are some examples of the questions on which students are graded and marked. Besides being irrelevant and missing the big ideas of Shakespeare and the atrocities that occurred during that first global massacre, students' future lives are being determined by their answers. What's wrong with that picture?

One reason that such "right answer" tests are so prevalent is that they are easy to mark. If the teacher has in mind the correct answers, then it is simply a matter of the teacher's eyeballing the page and indicating in red pencil which the wrong answers are, summing up the total correct and putting a mark or grade at the top of the page. Easy peasy. But of what educational value?

The end result is that the student only knows his or her mark; hardly an indication of what he or she has to do to improve, to further understanding, to gain access to the next rung on the ladder. Never mind the quality of learning that such tests support. If one can call it learning.

If all of those substantiated failings of the marking and grading system are not enough to persuade any doubter as to their inherent lack of value and their distortion of the important goals of education, there are at least two more worth mentioning.

At its best, evaluation of a student's work is meant to give that student feedback to enable his or her further growth, further understanding, further skill. In other words, "here's what is wrong with this work and here is what you need to do in order to improve." For that surely is the primary goal of education, the primary consideration of evaluation.

But there is no meaning in a mark or grade at the top of a paper; the student only learns where he or she ranks in the hierarchy of class performance. There may be spelling errors that are pointed out; there may be miscalculations in doing addition and subtraction examples; there may be a B+ at the top of an English essay—but how does that inform the learner? What does he or she have to do to improve understanding and to do better next time? This huge failure of this impoverished system does a disservice to students and to teachers as well.

Marks and grades on a student's record do not, in any way, reveal that student's intrinsic worth as a scholar, as a student, as a learner. They provide no important information other than the rank, however suspect, at which he or she sits on the classroom scale.

And finally, we come to the notion of the amount of time allotted for students to write a test, or finish a task, as if speed, or adherence to performing according to the arbitrary test time, is an important measure of a student's competence. There are some very intelligent, competent, and wise people who are notoriously "slow processors." They take more time to read, to consider, to sit down and actually complete a task. This doesn't mean that they are less smart; they are merely slower at doing something important. Should they be penalized for being "slow processors?"

If "thinking takes time," and if the time for thinking normally varies from person to person, why has it become essential for all students to complete a task in a given amount of time specified by the powers that be who established such odd rules? Given time specifications, students who race to finish may do better, while students who need time to mull over, consider, think carefully, reflect, are penalized. Wherever did such "rules" for assessing students' work come from?

Perhaps the origins of the need for speed in performance lie also in the nineteenth century, when the Ford Motor Company introduced its first assembly line, and speed was closely related to product completion and thus profit? While that reason does not hold in education, the time factor in students' completion of tasks remains a constant in how the student is being evaluated.

The arguments against the current and deeply entrenched marking and grading system in schools, from the kindergarten to the university, are legion, and the system persists despite the efforts of many researchers, writers, and educators who declaim against them (Kohn, 2012; Durm, 1993; Finkelstein, 1913; Bok, 2006; Hoffman, 1964; Owen, 1985; Gould, 1981; Kirschenbaum, Napier and Simon, 1971; Wilhelms and Diederich, 1967). Is it another case of perpetuating a flawed system because "we always did it that way?" What does it take to change a defective system and use, instead, evaluation practices that aid and abet student learning and enable them to take the next steps on the ladder of improvement?

This writer does not want to see the end of evaluating students' work. This book instead suggests an alternative approach—one that is more true to the professed goals of education—the enabling of student learning. Marks and grades have a very bad record of not doing that, but there are alternatives, and many suggestions for improved evaluation practices are included in the chapters that follow. It's a matter of keeping our means consistent with our goals.

Is that too much to ask?

Chapter 3

A Case for Using Evaluative Feedback

A teacher must have love, even for the bad ones. (Robert M., grade 6)

Chapter 2 has offered extensive arguments about the failings of the marking and grading systems used, in perpetuity, in classrooms from the early grades through the academy. This chapter attempts to make a case for the importance of using evaluative feedback to inform students and parents of not only what is lacking in students' work but provides them with the means of understanding what they need to do to improve. Surely this is a primary goal of teaching and learning for "once the burden of grade/record production is lifted, there is freedom for something very different. The teacher's key question can shift from what a pupil's grade should be to what it is that the student needs to know about his work and about himself" (Wilhelms and Diederich, 1967).

At the very first, it is important to recognize and affirm a little appreciated goal of evaluation: it is, after all, to enable and encourage learners to become more skilled as self-evaluators. If students remain wedded to the need for external affirmation, or for looking to others to determine their competence and their shortcomings, they will, even as adults, be looking outside of themselves, because they lack a most important and significant condition of adulthood: maturity and self-knowledge.

The worst-case scenario is when a person has become entirely dependent on that outside affirmation, seeking, manipulating others to give it, craving it so badly as to force situations into providing it. When that fails to come, the person in the process is devastated, so great is the need. And when it does come, it does not last; those needs for outside affirmation are never fully satisfied. It may not be farfetched to suggest that the great need for outside affirmation is at the root of much sycophantic behavior.

Carl Rogers (1961) was arguably one of the first to write about the importance of the relationship between a person's values and standards that are dependent upon the judgments and expectations of others, or on that person's own values and standards that are based upon a reliance upon his or her own experiences. Rogers has written that "the most fundamental condition of creativity is that the source or locus of evaluative judgment is internal. The value of his product is, for the creative person, established not by the praise or criticism of others, but by himself" (Rogers, 1961).

Or, as some wag noted, "What would Beethoven's music be like, or Picasso's paintings and sculpture, if these men had succumbed to the blistering judgments of their critics?"

What does the ability to be one's own self-evaluator look like in everyday behavior? Is that kind of behavior something we prize? Aspire to? Believe to be important in mature and independent-thinking adults? According to Rogers, these adults make choices and establish values according to their own thoughtfully examined beliefs. They will behave in ways that are less defensive, more socially responsible. They behave in ways that are regarded as more mature, and irrational and infantile ways of behaving will rarely be seen (Rogers, 1961).

How does it benefit us, as adults, to be in charge of our own self-assessments? To be able, for ourselves, to determine where we need to improve and where we excel? To be able, nondefensively to admit that we were wrong and need help? To be able to see ourselves without an overly inflated view of our successes and accomplishments?

"Diagnostic teaching takes the learner-as-person into account as much as the technicalities of content. It gives him rich opportunities to learn about himself and to feel his way toward what he needs to learn. It helps him grow in self-acceptance and respect for his own intuitions" (Wilhelms and Diederich, 1967). It enables learners to incorporate this feedback into a valid and healthy image of self, to learn about their own strengths and resources, in a way that allows them to incorporate these into their self-concept. It enriches their vision of the opportunities and the choices that can be open to them, by being able to appraise, realistically, their weaknesses and the limitations of their own resources.

Students who develop such a sense of personal strength gain the psychological freedom to look with clear eyes at themselves. Those who are overwhelmed by a hopeless sense of failure are forced, for their own preservation, to distort the evidence and never become truly self-aware.

These goals go to the very private world of learners. Without that self-awareness, maturity, and ability to see themselves more clearly and nondefensively, they are cut off from chances to understand themselves and bring their own motivations to bear on their future learning.

EVALUATION AS FEEDBACK

The importance of evaluative feedback to the learner, at every step of the educational process, cannot be overestimated. It is at the very heart of learning. When effective, it is based on the reasoned analysis of what the teacher has perceived in the student's work, and what steps the student must take in order to improve. No one said this job was easy; for in some ways, it is akin to the primary care physician, who is asked, with the limited tools at his or her hands, to make a diagnosis of what the patient needs to take in order to restore health.

Listening, observing, perceiving, and intuiting—all of those skills are in play for the physician as they are for the teacher reading a student's work or observing a student's oral performance. All of those are taken into consideration in making a diagnosis of what is perceived as weakness or illness and what is perceived as strengths. And the feedback given can enable or injure.

Of course, the more experienced the teacher or the doctor is at doing this, the more successful they become at the task. Practice alone does not make perfect; it is the teacher or the doctor's ability to assess his or her own skill in executing these diagnoses and making, in retrospect, analysis of the feedback, to perceive and understand how better to do this the next time and the next. The teacher or diagnostician is his/her own self-evaluator.

When it comes to students' written work that lies in the area of "right and wrong," it is easier to make diagnosis of the errors. The feedback need not rest on numbers and letters; it may be given in a more helpful form. When the student's work lies in an area that wants more subjective diagnosis, it is helpful to reveal that it is the teacher's judgment, and not the truth.

I noticed that you are adding 2 + 2 and arriving at +5 as the sum. Can you use some "counters" and make sure about that?

In your essay about Jane Austen, I see that you have located her birth and death dates as 1875 to 1917. Can you check that again, please, and, perhaps give some indication of your perceptions of women writers in that time period?

I liked the story very much and it is my impression that you worked very hard on it. I'm having a little bit of trouble figuring out the motivation for the Emily's behavior and I'm wondering if you can write a little more about her to give the reader some insight into why she acted as she did?

These are some examples of how a teacher diagnoses the weaknesses and points to the ways in which the learner may tackle the next steps in moving forward in understanding and skill. In each case, the ball is kicked into the learner's court to figure out what he or she needs to do to improve. In each case, the feedback is done with appreciation for learner's sense of self—not to harm, not to insult, but to offer suggestions for improvement. In each case, the teacher "owns" his or her role as evaluator—in other words, "this is my opinion." Implicitly, it communicates that evaluation lies in the eye of the evaluator and is not truth.

It will be easy to see that this kind of evaluative comment takes more time from the teacher's precious day than merely putting a mark on the paper. That cannot be denied. And only a teacher can decide if the time to do this is worth it; in other words, what's the payoff for teachers and students who engage in this process? One teacher commented that, while resistant at first to undertaking this kind of commitment, he found, to his surprise, that he actually enjoyed the process more; that it became more of a learning experience for him and not the rote and mindless marking he had done in the past.

Chapters 4, 5, and 6 give more detailed information about diagnosis and feedback, with examples given across several grades and curriculum areas. The introductory comments above are the merest beginning of the conversation about diagnosis and feedback.

OBSTACLES TO USING EVALUATIVE FEEDBACK IN LIEU OF GRADES

Very few would argue against the value of using evaluative diagnostic feedback to promote and enable student learning. Yet, in too many schools across the continent, the preferences are for using grades in lieu of diagnostic reporting. It may be helpful to point to some of the reasons for this, in the hope that when such reasons are identified, there is more of a chance that they can be legitimately and rationally addressed.

One primary obstacle is the pressure on teachers, from administration, from school boards, from parents, to measure and judge. There is such a long and hard history of measuring in the school system, and the system is so ingrained as to make it seem immutable. How long, for example, did it take the medical profession to recognize Ludwig Semmelweiss's Germ Theory as a cause of childbed fever, when all he was asking was for doctors to wash their hands with a solution of chlorinated lime, before surgery? (The unhappy answer is two decades.)

So far, the grading system has endured much longer, despite the evidence attesting to its faults.

Another impediment to change is attributed to college entrance requirements. According to Wilhelms and Diederich (1967), "To put it bluntly, any system of evaluation and record keeping which failed to facilitate the entrance of a school's graduates into appropriate colleges would not have a ghost of a chance of surviving, no matter how ideal it may be in other respects."

But that excuse is not quite the case. First, college admission officers now look at much more than the grades students present on their records. They seek other evidence to demonstrate applicants' readiness to undertake higher-level course work, as well as their prepared written essays, and a record of their outside of school activities. So other significant data play an important role in the college admission acceptances.

The role parents play, especially those in upper-class communities where considerable emphasis is on student success and where grades and the ranking system that is part and parcel of grading, cannot be overestimated. There are highly vocal parents who want not information about their child's capabilities and learning needs, but more, an edge with respect to where their child stands in relation to others. In other words, grades become a bragging point for parents who are accustomed to wanting and getting the best. This is one unhealthy condition that, unhappily, is part of what keeps a flawed system alive.

To confront parents with the limitations of grades and to attempt to encourage them to see the better alternative in diagnostic evaluative feedback may be on the same level as trying to convince doctors, in 1847, to wash their hands. So deeply ingrained are some parental needs to have their children excel, to be at the top of the class, to earn the best marks, as to make them not very amenable to seeing alternatives. And that is a tough nut to crack.

But like all problems and impediments, there are ways around that too. To know the impediment, to give it a name and a voice, makes it possible to identify ways to deal with it.

There is one further impediment that needs mention, and that is the intrinsic value of teachers' diagnostic feedback—that is, to what extent is it a fair, or an "on target" representation of a student's difficulties and a fair and "on target" set of suggestions for improvement. Not all feedback meets those standards. The feedback needs to inform students, as well as parents, as to learning needs, and give specific suggestions for taking the next steps. It should also put the onus on the learner to take those steps.

In this case, it would be a matter of some professional development for teachers who have not been adequately trained to do this kind of work. And that is what chapters 4, 5, and 6 hope to accomplish.

In the final analysis, it is once again the teacher who decides what choices are to be made in evaluating students' work. There is, as it is said, "no free lunch." Every decision, every new teaching strategy, every new proposal to be considered is carefully and thoughtfully weighed. In making these tough decisions, it's hard to resist the promise of a quick fix, of buying into a scheme that is easy, but that does not fulfill the promise of making that difference. Perhaps the answer lies in the question that we teachers ask ourselves: Is this good? And if the answer is positive, perhaps we will be able to see a sea change in the ways in which students are aided, abetted, and encouraged to see evaluation not as a means of placing them in rank order, but as a tool to help them understand and become more skillful in advancing intellectually, academically and emotionally, not only in school, but in life.

Chapter 4

Evaluative Feedback that Enables and Promotes Growth

The starting point for a teacher's evaluative feedback to students (and parents) begins with the underlying principle that what is "fed back" should enable a student to determine where she or he is with respect to the standards, objectives and goals of the subject, or grade level that have been set by the school/district/state. To that end, evaluation procedures should meet at least the following criteria:

1. Evaluation practices should reflect the subject/grade level's overall goals and objectives. That is, student progress should be assessed against the learning standards for that subject/grade.
2. Evaluation should allow for identifying student learning needs and point to remediation or corrective teaching. That is, the feedback should be specific and clearly related to the student's more urgent learning needs.
3. Evaluation should emphasize the enablement of further student learning and de-emphasize comments that are hurtful to students' concepts of self. For example, it should be informative and not cruel, helpful and not harmful, and enabling and not crushing.
4. Evaluation practices should allow that the feedback is not "truth," but one person's view of what needs correcting or editing, modification or improvement.
5. The teacher's feedback should not attempt to assess every detail in the student's work, emphasizing primarily the more important issues.
6. The teacher's feedback should recognize that the nature of a performance is variable, that is, every one of us has a "bad day." A student's overall competence should be assessed over time.
7. And finally, an essential part of the evaluative process should lead the student to become more skilled in self-evaluation, thus furthering the

process of the student's growing awareness of his and her own strengths and areas of needed growth. The teacher's feedback should enable the student to take the next steps on his or her own, thus promoting his or her independence as a learner.

With these principles in mind, the task of giving evaluative feedback becomes clearer. A check list for teachers is a handy tool to keep these principles in mind:

CHECKLIST FOR GIVING EVALUATIVE FEEDBACK

- Have I given the student a clear idea of what needs further examination in his or her work?
- Have I made my feedback clear, and unambiguous?
- Have I indicated how the work meets the grade/subject standards?
- Have I identified what's important for the student to consider in making the changes in his or her work?
- Have I not committed the sin of "overkill" in assessing everything in the work, emphasizing primarily the important issues?
- Have I a clear appreciation of what's important in my assessment of the student's work?
- Have I identified the next steps I believe the student should take in furthering his or her understanding and/or skill?
- Have I given the student clear direction in my feedback to enable him or her to "fix" what needs fixing on his or her own?
- Have I given feedback in such a way that the learner's sense of self is not diminished by what I have said or written?
- Have I indicated to the student that the feedback is my view, rather than truth?
- Have I taken into consideration that a student's performance on an oral or written task is variable, that there are some good days and some not so good days?
- Have I provided opportunity for the learner to give his and her ideas of how the work may be improved, promoting the learner's skill as a self-evaluator?
- Have I avoided unhelpful comments, such as "good" and "needs more work"?

These are hardly the be all and end all of guidelines for giving evaluative feedback, but it is surely a strong beginning.

And there's one more thing, and this may be the most shocking principle of all: not every piece of written work or oral presentation needs to be evaluated. The teacher is in a position to choose which items should be given evaluative scrutiny and which can be safely left unremarked. Too much evaluation can be soul destroying for teachers as well as for students; teachers don't need to follow the dictum: if it moves, test it.

IDENTIFYING THE CRITERIA: WHAT ARE WE LOOKING FOR?

In the elementary grades, teachers are faced with having to evaluate students' papers across a range of subject areas. That means that teachers not only have to attend to the principles above but also have to apply different criteria for reading and assessing students' papers in different subject areas. For example, in written papers in which single correct answers are called for, the criteria are clear. In written work where more subjective feedback is required, teachers need to be clear about the criteria being used to make the assessments and ensure that the criteria are applied consistently and fairly for each student. When teachers are clear about the standards underlying the assessments, evaluative feedback comes a bit easier.

For example, playing wrong notes in a piano performance is one clear indication of one set of standards that is being assessed. That is not the only standard of musical performance. More subjective standards include "musicality" and nuance of phrasing and expression, and attention to the style of the composer.

In a student's written work, incorrect information, wrong dates, misspellings, sentence structure, punctuation error—these are clear and unambiguous. When it comes to more subjective issues such as "narrative voice," or elegance of phrasing, or level of interest, or character development or other subjective issues, it is important that the feedback reveal the teacher's own assessment biases to indicate how, in that teacher's view, the feedback reflects one or more of the standards.

Examples of evaluative feedback that meet the criteria discussed above on prototypical students' written work are found in chapter 5.

WHAT IS BEING MEASURED?

It is no secret that teacher-made tests are notoriously full of ambiguous questions (e.g., "What are the three human races?"); questions that ask for recall of arcane information (e.g., "What was the name of the first chimp that was launched into space?"); questions that ask for erroneous information (e.g., "In what year did Shakespeare graduate from high school?"); questions that ask for simple answers to complex issues (e.g., "What were the three causes of World War I?"). These are not only examples of poor tests questions; they also incur and promote wrongful thinking about the nature of assessment, and the more fundamental question of what is important in learning.

In creating classroom tests, or measures of student learning, teachers need to be mindful of "what's important?" That is: What is it that I want to know about what my students have learned? What do I value about what they have learned? What information is relevant to me? What kinds of mental processes do I want to see in students' responses? All of these should be considered in the creation of classroom tests.

It is true that "single correct answer" tests are the easiest to mark. If that be the case and teachers are wedded to that kind of assessment, the test questions should, at the very least, reflect the important issues being studied, and not the trivial. It has been the experience of many teachers that emphasis on the recall of names, dates, and places do a disservice to the study of history and that they emphasize what is insignificant over what is essential. The bottom line in creating these short answer tests is that they call for what the teacher considers worth learning and remembering. The bad news is that it may be the case that no short answer question can do that job.

An alternative to the short answer test is to ask students to reflect on some important issues or important ideas that they have learned about in a particular topic, or theme, or episode and tell their "answers" in a classroom test. Such a question would be more than revealing; it would allow students to show and tell what they have learned about the issue, and what has been significant about that. It would also give teachers an idea of how students process information and how they deliver their responses—that is, the quality of their thinking as well as the substance of their learning. Finally, it would give teachers an idea of what has been successfully taught and what skills or concepts need further attention and for whom.

Not for the fainthearted is the idea that students provide teachers with some suggestions for test questions, which the teacher considers, and uses the best of them in the creation of a student/teacher-made test.

LEARNING GOALS AND EVALUATION PRACTICES

Since evaluation practices cannot take place in the absence of prior consideration of a program's or grade level's goals, an example of the learning goals of a middle-grade inquiry-oriented science program is offered below. This list of goals was created by a team of middle-grade teachers and is based upon school district guidelines as well as their own additions that reflect what they also consider important in an inquiry-oriented, hands-on science program. The goal statements provide the guidelines that inform evaluative feedback.

GOALS FOR A SCIENCE PROGRAM

Social

1. Increased growth in independent, responsible classroom behavior
2. Increased growth in the ability to make reasoned, thoughtful choices and acceptance of the consequences of one's decisions
3. Increased growth in being a socially responsible and cooperative participant of a group
4. Increased growth in assuming responsibility for the classroom learning environment
5. Increased growth as a purposeful, productive learner and group member

Personal and Ego

1. Increased awareness of self as an individual with strengths and limitations
2. Increased sense of self as an individual with power to manipulate one's environment
3. Increased awareness of one's own capabilities to function as a problem solver
4. Increased growth of personal pride in self as a competent and skilled participant of a group
5. Increased sense of personal autonomy and ego strength
6. Increased growth as a self-initiator
7. Increased sense of self-worth
8. Increased sense of self as a creator and a cognitive risk taker

Cognitive and Intellectual

1. Increased skills in making thoughtful, accurate observations
2. Increased skills in forming reasoned and appropriate hypotheses
3. Increased skills in identifying assumptions and differentiating assumptions from fact
4. Increased skills in making comparisons and in identifying similarities and differences
5. Increased skills in classifying objects and in creating categories in which various items may be ordered
6. Increased skills in gathering data and making meaningful interpretations of the data
7. Increased skills in making decisions based on reasoned deliberation and thoughtful consideration of alternatives
8. Increased skills in creating, imagining, and inventing
9. Increased ability to be more tolerant of uncertainty
10. Increased skills in designing projects and experiments to test hypotheses

11. Increased ability to formulate and raise questions about phenomena
12. Increased understanding of the "big" scientific concepts
13. Increased knowledge base with respect to scientific information

Appreciations and Attitudes

1. Increased appreciation for science as a means of acquiring information and understanding the world and the universe
2. Increased love for science and scientific explorations
3. Increased joy in exploration, in searching, in experimentation for discovery
4. Increased ability to recognize science as a process of discovering rather than a body of information with accepted "truths."[1]

When the goals are identified, it becomes clear that such outcomes cannot be measured simply and certainly not with any single pencil-and-paper test, no matter how sophisticated. Nor can such a comprehensive view of pupil growth be reflected in a single-numerical score. In fact, no pencil-and-paper test is likely to be more effective in diagnosing how well students meet the goals of the science program than the day-to-day professional observations of a teacher.

Close scrutiny of student behavior, in a variety of tasks, over an extended period of time, such as observing student interactions in a group, observing student problem-solving abilities on given tasks, and noting where and how difficulties arise for that student, will uncover valuable data about student ability and learning. Teachers' professional observations cannot be over-rated as a source of the richest data for assessment. In spite of the potential for personal bias, the wealth of data from teacher observations is likely to be infinitely more reliable to the classroom teacher in promoting student learning than any numerical score on any single examination.

How a teacher chooses to assess student learning, and what standards the teacher uses to make those assessments are key factors in evaluating students' work. In the best of circumstances, the feedback should at least, be cognizant of the important criteria for evaluating learning. The feedback should also reflect the relationship between the student's performance and the program or subject-area goals. In the overall, evaluative feedback should be honest, fair, and enabling. That is the least it should be able to do.

NOTE

1. (Reprinted with permission of the publisher, from Selma Wassermann and J. W George Ivany, *The New Teaching Elementary Science: Who's Afraid of Spiders?* New York: Teachers College Press, 1996. All rights reserved.)

Chapter 5

Written Diagnostic Evaluative Feedback across the Curriculum

> *"How do you suppose those mountains got so big?" the teacher asks her group of six-year-olds.*
> *Simon sits quietly and puts his head down. "I don't know."*
> *"Well, perhaps you have some theories about it?" she encourages him to reconsider.*
> *Simon lifts his head and looks into the distance. "Well, I think they began like little stones and grew and grew until they grew up and became mountains."*
> *"Ah. I see. Thank you for giving us your theory."*

The assessment of students' work can be a powerful tool for the good. Used wisely, by informed teachers, it can enable students to take the next steps in improving their work. It can help students to see what needs modification, elaboration, correction. It can promote students' thinking about what they have written or said, and further their examination of the process by which they have arrived at their conclusions. It can elevate and enable the process of self-evaluation.

Used unwisely, cavalierly, or in an unenlightened way, it can be soul crushing.

Of course, there are many ways of giving evaluative feedback—none of which is "truth." The act of assessment lies in the eye of the beholder. In that sense, it is important that the evaluator indicate that this is his or her perspective, not a judgment writ in stone. Teachers will bring their own points of view about a student's work into the fore; they will also consider the developmental stage of the student in giving that feedback. Some will also consider the effect of the feedback on the student's progress.

Feedback to a child in the primary years is, of necessity, a different kind. It will have a different tone and raise different questions than feedback to a student in the upper grades. The teacher is also the arbiter of how and whether to pursue the matter further, or just let the issue drop. Like so many things that teachers do, "it depends." In short, it depends on many factors that enter into a teacher's consideration of how the feedback is going to affect the student and how it will enable his or her further learning.

To facilitate understanding about the how and the what of evaluative assessment as feedback and guide, a number of examples are offered in the sections below. The student papers included have been gathered by teachers, administrators, and parents and offered for use in this text. Approval from the students has also been obtained, and although their names are absent from the papers themselves, their contributions have been noted in the acknowledgments. In each instance, a rationale for the teacher's feedback is given.

Working with the "real stuff" from classrooms offers the best examples of how students perform on written tasks across a variety of subject areas and across several grade levels, as well as being cognizant of the principles cited in chapter 4.

One teacher who received a "teaching excellence" award claimed that one of his strategies in giving student feedbacks was never to use a red pencil. Another teacher using evaluative feedback said she wrote in pencil, so she could erase a word, a sentence, a thought, if, upon reconsideration, it seemed inappropriate.

EXAMPLES FROM THE PRIMARY GRADES ACROSS THE CURRICULUM

There are no biological creatures more wonderful than young children. A living, breathing set of paradoxes, they are at once both in the present and in the future. They are full of sweet innocence, yet crafty as old con artists. Outrageously silly, yet deadly serious. Short on experience, yet unequivocal about what they know. Gently loving and demoniacally mischievous. Fiercely independent, yet afraid of monsters. Unself-conscious, yet needing adult approval. They are vigorous, demanding, excessive, frustrating, and exhausting, but never boring. What's more, their capacity to be frank is disconcerting.

I bought you this handkerchief for a present. Don't you dare blow your nose in it. It cost $2.00.

Evaluative feedback to younger children in the primary years must nurture those precious qualities, while at the same time allowing and encouraging them to take the next steps to maturity.

1. An original story from Maya, an emerging reader, early grade 1

Moon Beam and the montin by Maya
Wuns a pona tim there wa a mucey. It wus cold
Moonbeam he had a grait famley
A man tuc him to a montin
It wus beie Moonbeam wus
Ce is Moonbeam went on the motin.
The end

Teacher's response:

Dear Maya

I liked your story about Moonbeam very much. I see the way you spelled your words according to how they sound to you. I am having some trouble reading some of the words and I wonder if you could come and read your story to me. Then maybe I can help you with some new spelling.

Response analysis:

The teacher appreciates Maya's work and points out her use of emergent spelling in her writing. She invites Maya to read the story to her, as a way of communicating her difficulty in reading some of the words and offers to help her with new spelling. The teacher deliberately avoids correcting the misspelled words in her story in the belief that emergent spelling is just a beginning in decoding the written word and that there will be many other opportunities to help Maya with correct spelling. As well, to point out every misspelled word would be crushing. Maya is instead appreciated for her efforts.

2. From Samantha, a student in grade 2

Tooker the Remarkable Dog, by Samantha
Once a upon a time there was a frog name
Lili. She moved. Now she has no friends to play with.
No friends said lili. I have no won to play with.
Then lili saw a dog chicken and a monkey.
Why do you and your friends have a t on your shrit.
Because the t mean we go to the tree house
Can I go to your treehouse
Yes. Yes.
You may go to are house.

Teacher's response:

Dear Samantha

I read your story about Lili, the frog who had just moved and who had no friends. She wanted to be friends with the monkey, the dog and the chicken who had a tree house. I'd like to know more about how to make friends when you move to a new place. Come and tell me what you think, and I can help you with some of your spelling.

> Response analysis:
>
> The teacher reflects the main ideas of the story back to Samantha and extends her thinking about how new friends are made and offers to help her with her spelling. To provide help with spelling is considered a wiser strategy than marking up the misspelled words on her story.

3. From Sven, grade 2

Fire pervention week. Don't leave old rages out they may catch on fire.

Teacher's response:

Hi Sven

Thank you for reminding us about how to keep our homes safe from fires. Can you have another look at the words *pervention* and *rages* and check them to see if the spelling is correct? Let me know.

> Response analysis:
>
> The teacher acknowledges Sven's thoughtfulness in pointing out a method for preventing fires and asks that he reconsider the spelling of two words. Instead of "marking them wrong," the teacher asks Sven to reexamine them and make the necessary changes.

4. Sylvie, grade 2

I know how to make Brown rice. First you cook your rice and then you put your chocolate and then you put sugar. And then you haft to whate.

Teacher's response:

Hi Sylvie. What happens when you mix the brown rice with the chocolate and the sugar? What does it taste like? Can you put that idea in your story too? How long do you have to wait?

Response analysis:

The teacher deliberately ignores the misspelled words in Sylvie's story and instead asks her to reflect on the outcome of her recipe as well as on the amount of time one must wait for results. Instead of marking the words wrong, the teacher knows that there will be other opportunities to help Sylvie with her spelling. What is being encouraged here is Sylvie's thoughtfulness about what she is advocating so that she may reflect more about the writing process.

5. Maya, age 8, learning about metaphors

Peace is like smelling lavender on a summer day.

Teacher's response:

Dear Maya

I loved your metaphor that described the smell of lavender in the summer. I think that is very original thinking on your part. I can't wait to see more of your work on metaphors.

Response analysis:

The teacher appreciates the quality of Maya's work, emphasizing her imaginative use of metaphor. The teacher "owns" the judgment as her own view of the work.

6. Rebecca, grade 2

Stars are soft because there made out of gas. Did you ever look into the fireplace. The wite is hot if you ever got burnt the blue is second hot but the red is not so hot.

Teacher's response:

Dear Rebecca

I liked your story about stars very much. You explained about how some colors are related to how hot things are—like white being very hot, and red being not so hot. I wonder how you figured that out. And how you figured out that stars are made of gas. Can you tell me about it?

Response analysis:

The teacher "owns" the evaluative feedback indicating that it is her own view of the work and reflects the use of imagery that relates temperature to color. She also asks Rebecca to think more about the idea that stars are made of gas, thus opening up further inquiry about them. She uses correct spelling of the misspelled words as feedback to Rebecca instead of red-penciling them on her paper.

7. From William, age 7

"A Story. If I was a space creature I would have antennas on my head. I would live in a crator on the moon. I would be green and I'd have my own flying saucer and I have eye lashes. And I'd play tricks on you."

Teacher's response:

Dear William

I see the way you used quotations at the beginning and the end of your story and I wonder what those quotations mean to you. Can you explain it to me? And I loved the way you used an apostrophe in the word I'd—to show that it is a contraction of the words "I would." That is a very grown up way of writing. I think your story has a lot of imagination and I'd like to see some more of your stories. Can you check the spelling of the word "crator" to be sure that you spelled it correctly?

> Response analysis:
>
> The teacher reflects back to William his use of quotes and asks William to reconsider what they represent, thus opening up inquiry about the use of quotation marks. She also affirms his more mature use of the apostrophe in word contractions. She "owns" her response, indicating that it is her own judgment and asks William to check the spelling of the word "crator."

8. Sonia, aged 7 (spoken response to her experiments with ice cubes)

I think the ice cube is going to melt faster when you crush it. I used the timer to see how long it takes. It melts faster when you crush it. Little drops of water are there already. But if you put it on the heat you'd really get some melting.

Teacher's oral response to Sonia:

You did some experiments to see if crushed ice would melt faster than ice cubes and you used your timer to see if your theory was right. You also said that if the ice was heated, it would melt even faster. How did you figure out that crushed ice would melt faster than ice cubes? Can you tell me your theory about it?

Response analysis:

The teacher reflects back to Sonia her ideas about ice melting faster when crushed and when heated and asks her to extend her thinking about how she came to those conclusions. The teacher's response is "value free" as interest in Sonia's thinking is deemed more important than a value judgment about what she has done.

9. Craig, age 8

We put some rocks in the bucket of water. It turned a different color.
To float a rock we can put a plastic bag under the rock. We choosed two rocks and they were different because they were not the same color or size.

Teacher's response:

Hi Craig. You are describing your experiments with sinking and floating things, testing out theories about which things float and which things sink. You tried to figure out how to turn a sinker to a floater and you had some ideas to test again. Come and tell me what happened when you finished your experiments and what you figured out about sinking and floating things.

Response analysis:

In giving Craig's feedback about his science experiment report, the teacher concentrates on Craig's growing awareness of buoyancy and encourages his further testing of his ideas. In the teacher's response, she considers that generating reflection about his ideas is more important than the lesser issue of correct spelling. No value judgments are necessary in encouraging further scientific investigation.

10. Heather, age 8, reporting on her scientific investigations

Me and Amerjeet put the eyedropper in the beaker. We put the balloon on the beaker. When me and Amerjeet prest the balloon the eyedropper went down and bubbles came out. We had lots of fun at the divers center.

Teacher's response:

Hi Heather. I'm wondering if you have a theory to explain what happened to make the bubbles come out when the eyedropper went down. Do you suppose it had something to do with air? Can you and Amerjeet come and talk to me about your ideas? I'm so glad you had fun at the Divers center.

Response analysis:

The teacher deliberately ignores misspelled words and grammatical structure and instead emphasizes what is more important in these children's scientific inquiries—that is, the nature of their theory building, based upon their investigations in the science centers. She calls for further thinking about how air might be a factor in producing the results the children observed and invites their further discussions with her about their ideas.

11. Bobby, age 7 (oral response)

I can't do this work. It's too hard on my brain.

Teacher's response:

Thank you for coming to tell me about how hard this work is for you. Let me see how I can help you. Try to tell me where you are having trouble.

Analysis of response:

The teacher acknowledges Bobby's difficulties with his work and offers help. She does not make a judgment or diminish his feelings about himself as a learner.

12. Keith, age 7

My desk is 18 inches long.
Its width is 14 inches.
The legs are 20 inches long.
The height is 24 inches.

Teacher's response:

Hi Keith:
I see that you have finished your measurements of your desk. I have some questions for you about them. Claudia measured her desk and had different results than you did. I wonder if you and Claudia could compare your measurements and come and tell me what you found.

Response analysis:

The teacher does not tell Keith that his measurements are wrong. Instead, she asks him to compare measurements with another student and then report on his findings. This encourages his own solution to the errors and opens up further inquiry about human error in measurement.

EXAMPLES FROM THE INTERMEDIATE GRADES ACROSS THE CURRICULUM

While the primary grade child is enchanting, bewildering, and full of surprises, the intermediate child has other capital. Older children have a greater capacity to understand. "Don't disturb us unless it is an emergency" is a clear directive that needs no extensive explanation. Their vocabulary base is large and the range of their experiences greater. They have seen the Grand Canyon and can speak knowledgeably of its depth.

They have become über skilled at using "tablets" and are sometimes referred to as the "tablet generation." In fact, their skill and knowledge about the Internet, apps, and tablets are so extensive and rich that in some cases, they exceed that of many adults. They are wise in their years; they know that there is no Santa Claus but will still cling to idealistic hopes of what a superhero can do in righting the world's wrongs.

The older elementary child is a many-splendored gift. Personal identities and values have become more solidly formed. They are much more wary in their acceptance of adults; you must work to win their affection and respect. But having won their hearts, they are exceedingly loyal, unremittingly generous. "My teacher said so" is the arbiter of the highest court, the final word at the dinner table.

These attributes of intermediate children bear on the evaluative feedback found in the examples below.

1. Joanna, grade 4

What is GREEN?
Green is long grass swaying in the empty meadow on the last day of summer break seeing the last sunset.
Green sound like aqua waves in Greece splashing repeatedly in one deriction to the other.
Green is sour taisting healthy but at the same time good.
Green is breath mints in the morning when your walking to school
It is bumpy like nature and very delicate
It's easy to rip apart. Green is only fresh in summer and spring
Green is allergies in spring when flowers bloom
It is leaving school on a Friday. Green is your birthday coming up in a couple of weeks

Green is spring when trees ar alive
Green is the husband to yellow with the son of blue.

Teacher's response:

Dear Joanna
I enjoyed your descriptions of the color green. To me, they are very imaginative, and they evoke some powerful images. I believe you are becoming a very gifted writer. I want to teach you now about proofreading your work and how you can do that kind of editing job that good writers do.

> Response analysis:
>
> The teacher shows "ownership" of his feedback indicating that it is his opinion and he highlights the creativity of her descriptions. Instead of marking the spelling and punctuation, he wants to teach her about proofreading and editing her own work—the next step for her to take as a growing writer.

2. Bob, grade 6

A good teacher must have patients with the children and parents at conferences when they don't understand something. They must have good humor and laugh when something is funny, but they have to be strict sometimes. They must always have confidence in the children, show them and lead them on the right road to succus. They be able to hold their temper and to the child in a nice way. Not only do they teach from book but in ways of making it fun to do it. They must know what work a child needs otherwise it makes it bad for him or her. They must always have love even for the bad ones.

Teacher's response:

Hi Bob. I appreciated your descriptions of what a good teacher is and what the teacher has to do to help children learn. You have pointed to some important characteristics—like having patience, having confidence, and holding their temper. I liked your idea that a good teacher should love all the children, even those who do not behave well. Thank you for those ideas. There are a few spelling errors in your paper and I am wondering if you need help in looking for them and correcting them. Let me know.

> Response analysis:
>
> The teacher recognizes Bob's not so subtle reference to the idea of a teacher caring for children who are "bad"—and wants to convey to him her

acknowledgement of the importance of that—since the reference is clearly to himself. She doesn't "mark' the incorrect spelling but invites him to look for the spelling errors himself and offers help if he needs it.

3. Mark, grade 6

I know that we eat protozoa, because you said that meat has cells and we eat meat, so we eat protozoa.

Teacher's response:

Hi Mark. I see you are making a comparison with meat, cells and protozoa. I'm wondering if you can take a few minutes and look up the definitions of the words: meat, protozoa, and cells and let me know what you find.

Response analysis:

The teacher sees this as an example of the kind of thinking that is described as "missing the meaning" and tries to give Mark some direction to help him see the differences in the terms so that he can, himself, correct his thinking about the relationships of these terms. She invites him to discuss his findings with her, giving her a chance to give him additional feedback if necessary.

4. Joyce, grade 4 (writing her impressions of an artist's sketch of the Golden Gate Bridge)

The Golden Gate Bridge. I see a splash of water and the bridge is red theirs two same line things that are red too. I wonder why they put it there. There is know arch or trestle. The water looks very blue and fresh of littles creatures, like fishes and more. I think it is a long way to go to another side cause it is over a big ocean The sky is blue just like the water and white for the clouds. You can see the shadow of the bridge and on the bridge are cars I wonder if the artise drew the picture cause it had a good view of everything like the water, bridge and the shadows. Probably in the water are fishes and on the water are barrows.

Teacher's response:

Hi Joyce. From reading your description of the picture, I see you had a strong impression of the Golden Gate Bridge, how long it was, how it spanned across a large body of water, and how the shadow of the bridge was seen on the water's surface. I found your descriptions thoughtful and imaginative and I liked the way you noted important details. I'm suggesting you proofread your paper and see if you can pick out the words that need correcting. If you need help to do that, please come and see me.

Response analysis:

The teacher "owns" her evaluative feedback in suggesting that these are his views. He identifies what he considers to be the strong points made by Joyce in her descriptions and praises the thoughtfulness of Joyce's views and her attention to detail. He asks her to proofread her work and puts the responsibility for identifying misspelled words on her, but also invites her to come for help if needed. Learning to proofread one's work is one factor in this teacher's emphasis on creative writing.

5. Harold, grade 6

Harold's math paper was returned to him with numerous errors in computation which were unmarked. Instead, the teacher made the following comments:

Teacher's response:

Hey Harold. I note that you are having trouble with computation on this math paper and I'm wondering if you need some help here. Think about how you arrived that those answers and sign up for a math conference with me if you need my help. If not, please review your work and submit the paper to me again. Thanks, Harold.

Response analysis:

The teacher recognizes Harold's ongoing difficulty with computation in math, and instead of marking his errors wrong, asks him to review the work himself, and resubmit the paper, also inviting him to come for help if he feels he needs it.

6. Max, grade 5

Things that weigh about 1 lb. and things that weigh about 1 K

Reading book	About 1 lb.	Less than 1 K.
Tin of nails	Over 1 lb.	About 1 K.
Tin of buttons	Less than 1 lb.	Less than 1 K.
6 pencils	Less than 1 lb.	less than 1 K.
Bucket of sand	More than 1 lb.	More than 1 K.
Glass of water	Less than 1 lb.	Less than 1 K.

Some sets of things that are sold in pounds are apples, pears, plums, cabbages, potatoes, sugar, cherries and carrots. They are also sold in kilograms in some stores.

Teacher's response:

Hi Max. You were doing some investigations involving weights. You calculated weights using the metric system and the imperial system. What are some discoveries you made about weights using imperial pounds and metric kilograms? Can you describe them?

Response analysis:

The teacher reflects back to Max the nature of his investigations into weights by pounds and kilograms. She extends his thinking, asking for him to consider the differences in the two systems.

7. Sophie, grade 4

Task: Show these as whole numbers:

1 ten and 5 ones
1 ten and 2 ones
2 tens and 7 ones
4 tens
3 tens and 5 ones
1 hundred
1 hundred two tens and 5 ones
I caint do it its to hard fr me.

Teacher's response:

Hi Sophie. I see you are having trouble with this work. Please come and see me and I will help you.

Response analysis:

The teacher does not condemn Sophie's inability, but rather acknowledges Sophie's difficulties with the assignment. The teacher understands Sophie's need for individual help and invites her to come for help.

8. Tommy, grade 6

Stealing is a bad thing because if you are caught stealing you will go to jail and your father will have to bail you out. One time I stole lollipops when I was a little boy. I put them in my pocket and walked out of the store. My mother didn't know it. And so I got free lollipops for nothing but I will never do that again because I realize it now.

Teacher's response:

Hi Tommy. You have chosen to write about something you did when you were a little boy and I think it was very brave of you to share that with me. Looking back now at what you did then reminds you about why it is wrong to steal from others—and the reasons are more than being caught. I wonder if you can tell me now about what some of those reasons are?

> Response analysis:
>
> The teacher acknowledges the risk Tommy has taken in sharing that event with his teacher. She applauds his braveness in doing so, and also extends his thinking about some of the moral issues involved.

9. Ricky, grade 6

Franklin and I made a model of the circulatory system. We used a large piece of cardboard and draw an outline of a human. Then we used colored plastic tubing to show the veins and arteries pumping blood to and from the heart. We had a pump stuck to the back of the figure and when we turned it on the water was pushed up and down the plastic tubing. The arteries had red tubing and the veins had blue tubing. But when we showed our project to the class, the tubing broke and water went all over. And everyone laughed.

Teacher's response:

I thought the project you did with Franklin showed a lot of creativity and inventiveness. I think it gave the other students a good idea of how the circulatory system works, even though the tubing broke and water spilled over the floor! I hope you and Franklin continue your science investigations as this seems to me to be an area of study that you both enjoy. Take a look at your report again and note the word "draw"—perhaps that is a typo?

Response analysis:

The teacher compliments Ricky on his and Franklin's work on the science project, indicating that it is her own view of it. She encourages them to consider other investigations, as this seems to be an area of study that they both enjoy and wants to extend to them opportunities to further their knowledge and skills. She also points out the error in the word "draw" asking the student to examine it and perhaps correct it.

10. Kiera, grade 4

My favrit part is when Ephraim, Mallory and Will go in to the tunles. They go to try to open the door and it just opens using the key from Mallorys mom.

Teacher's response:

Hi Kiera. I see that you have described your favorite part of the story—the part you liked best. I am wondering why you enjoyed that part so much. Can you write about that too? I'd like to point out two words that you might want to add to your personal dictionary: favorite, and tunnels. And if you remember about using an apostrophe to show "possession," check the word Mallorys.

Response analysis:

The teacher acknowledges Kiera's report and invites her to extend her thinking about the reason for that part of the story to have been her favorite. She points out two misspelled words and suggests Kiera add them to her personal dictionary. She also refers Kiera to the work the class did on using the apostrophe and suggests Kiera check back on her treatment of the word Mallorys.

EXAMPLES FROM THE SECONDARY SCHOOL ACROSS THE CURRICULUM

A brief visit to Terry Fox Secondary school gives a microscopic view of what it's like to teach students at this level of their intellectual, social, and emotional development.

The students linger in corridors in thick clusters, laughing, comparing events in their lives, giving advice, embracing, kissing. The dress code is informal, hair styles conforming to idiosyncratic tastes, from the nearly bald, to the more carefully coiffed. There is no urgency to their movements; no one seems to be in a hurry to get to class.

A few fourteen- and fifteen-year-old girls are pushing baby carriages, which will be deposited in a school day care center while the teen mothers are in class. The students seem both sophisticated and immature. They hover between two worlds, that of emerging adult and adult. Most of them by now are their own "masters," knowing what they want; others are still unsure. While their sophistication is skin deep, they demand to be treated as adults.

They are quick to tell a teacher about his or her shortcomings, unafraid to show their disdain, all the while wanting and needing that teacher's respect. And of course, most, if not all, of them are glued to their cell phones, their tablets, the Internet, Facebook, YouTube, and their social networks. If they are not quite mature, they are sophisticates in the IT world.

The range of maturity and intellectual levels is wider and deeper at these ages; some students show expertise, even brilliance in their work, while others struggle to make sense of basic concepts.

More than a few of them, by this time of their lives, have already chosen their career pathways. Others are unsure, undecided, uncertain. Some are deeply wedded to parental values; others have broken ranks and declared their independence.

The teacher who "knows" and "understands" all of this, who knows about students who carry a load of hostility, who are unresponsive, whose responses are lackluster, arrogant, defensive—will have, at his or her command, the resources and skills to deal with such a range of talents, behaviors and attitudes. No one said it was easy. But then, what teaching job is?

Yet, teachers who have long experience in teaching secondary students would never think of teaching at any other level. For when deep and abiding relationships are formed, they are likely to endure for all time.

1. Adam, grade 11 (social studies)

It was absolutely right that the U.S. interned the Japanese during World War II. Even though they were citizens, they bombed Pearl Harbor and so they were dangerous and had to be imprisoned.

Teacher's response:

You have read the material and have come to the conclusion that the US government was justified in interning US citizens because they were of Japanese descent. The reason you give is that these citizens were responsible for the bombing of Pearl Harbor. Since the bombing was carried out by the naval and air force of Japan, and not by those US citizens, how do you support your idea?

> Response analysis:
>
> This is a difficult one to evaluate because the roots of that thinking lie in the student's evident bias. To confront it head on would likely cause defensiveness. The teacher has chosen, instead to ask Adam to reconsider his idea, given the data he has provided, leaving the "door open" for further inquiry. The teacher makes note of this kind of thinking and will seek other opportunities to address it further down the line.

2. Sean, —grade 12 (English)

After seeing the film *Invictus*, the students are asked to describe how the poem Invictus helped Nelson Mandela to endure his suffering during his twenty-seven-year incarceration in South Africa.

This film has two themes. The first is the election of Mandela to the presidency of South Africa after Apartheid, during a time when there was still great racial tension, and how Mandela used the rugby team Springboks, to try to unite both blacks and whites in solidifying the country. The second theme is to show how Mandela took the team to his former prison and gave them hope that they could actually win. Invictus inspired Mandela to withstand his imprisonment and never to be defeated. If Invictus could sustain Mandela and give him hope to overcome, then Invictus could help the team to overcome their defeats and rise to victory.

Teacher's response:

Hi Sean. I liked the way you highlighted the two themes of the film, that is, the theme of Mandela's use of the Springboks to unite a racially divided country and the theme of how the poem Invictus helped Mandela to withstand his very long imprisonment. Can you be a bit more specific and give an example or two of what there is in the poem that you think is so inspiring?

> Response analysis:
>
> The teacher shows appreciation of what Sean has written in his essay, avoids making comments about grammar, and asks him to consider adding more material about the poem that would give greater meaning to his analysis. What's considered important is the nature of Sean's thinking and analysis more than his grammar.

3. Ellie, grade 10 (chemistry)

Assignment: The teacher provided a list of elements and asked students to construct categories under which they might be classified: hydrogen, uranium, lithium, magnesium, potassium, oxygen, aluminum, mercury, bromine, sulphur, chlorine, argon.

I can classify them according to if they are solid, liquid, or gas. I can classify them according to if they are metals or non-metals.

Teacher's response:

I see you have thought about two ways to classify these elements, Ellie. I'd like to see how you order them into these classifications as that would help me to understand your understanding of them. Can you do that?

> Response analysis:
>
> The teacher does not reprimand Ellie for her very limited response, but rather encourages her to extend her thinking by asking her to do the actual classifications so that her understanding of those elements is made clear to both of them.

4. Pham, grade 9 (biology)

The assignment is to compare the heart and the lungs, to find similarities and differences.

Similarities:

1. *body organs*
2. *necessary to keep body alive*
3. *located in upper half of body*
4. *expand and contract*
5. *made up of cells*
6. *contain compartments*
7. *have openings into tubes*

Differences:

Heart	Lungs
One organ	paired organ
Contains blood	contains air

Written Diagnostic Evaluative Feedback across the Curriculum 47

Contracts itself	forced to contract by pressure of diaphragm
No opening to outside of body	open to outside of body
Made of muscles	made of elastic tissue
Contains valves	no valves
Four compartments	many compartments
Eight openings into tubes	two openings into tubes

Teacher's response:

Hi Pham. I appreciate your thoughtful comparison of the heart and the lungs and I see you have included many critical features of both organs in your comparison. I'm wondering about the exclusion of the fact that both are essential for the body to function and the material used by each organ to perform that function. I'm also wondering about your idea that the lungs are "open to outside the body." Can you clarify that for me? Can you think about those points and let me know if you want to make any changes in your paper?

    Response analysis:

    The teacher acknowledges the work that Pham has done (he is a recently arrived new English learner) and asks him to consider additional points that seem to her to need further examination.

5. Ezra, grade 10 (History)

This is the timeline I have made for the beginning of time. About 120,000 B. C. the Neanderthal peoples lived in Europe and western Asia. They are called "homo sapiens" which means modern humans. Homo sapiens probably came from Africa. It took thousands of years later for more modern humans to appear. There were cave paintings on the walls of the caves and they tell about how people lived in caves and what tools they used in their lives. It's all very creepy and interesting.

Teacher's response:

Hi Ezra. Thank you for giving me your ideas about the earliest living humans on earth. You mention the Neanderthals who lived in Europe and western Asia, but I think you have misunderstood about "Homo sapiens," who came later and who evolved from their earlier ancestors, the Neanderthals. How were these two groups different?
    You also noted that scientists are able to tell about these early lives from the paintings on the walls of the caves. It would also be helpful for your timeline if you could provide some dates for more recent human development.

Response analysis:

The teacher appreciates Ezra's work on his timeline and asks him to go further in his study by noting the differences between Neanderthals and Homo sapiens. He also notes that Ezra has mentioned the use of cave drawings to give evidence of some of those early lives and asks for Ezra to complete work on his timeline.

6. Neil, grade 12 (biology)

The Spanish flu killed millions of people in less than a year. In fact, the Spanish flu was responsible for killing more people than World War I. That is why it is called the pandemic of 1918–1919.

How come the infection was so swift and so widespread? Maybe it was because they didn't get the word out about the disease. No Internet. Maybe it was because there wasn't enough medical supplies to treat the sick. There was no cure, and no vaccine. But I think it was because the doctors in charge did not know how dangerous the virus was, and how it spread so easily and quickly. They didn't even know it was a virus. So people with the infection traveled all over and spread the germs and there was no cure.

Teacher's response:

Hi Neil. I appreciated your description of the Spanish flu of 1918–1919 and how it decimated a huge number of people across the globe. I liked the way you pointed to some possible causes for that pandemic. You correctly point to the fact that doctors at that time did not know much about the virus and, in fact, were unable to locate the source of the disease. How do you suppose the electron microscope helps scientists today discover those minute organisms that cause disease? What's your theory about that? And given the data about the scarcity of medical knowhow at that time, what suggestions would you have made to doctors that might have contributed to the prevention of the spread of the disease?

Response analysis:

The teacher appreciates Neil's beginning understanding of what contributed to the spread of the Spanish flu. She raises the level of his thinking by asking him to hypothesize how an electron microscope might have helped scientists at that time discover the cause. She also extends his thinking by asking him how, using the data available at that time, the spread of the disease might have been prevented.

7. Debbie, grade 10 (earth science)

Don't kill worms! They are a gardener's best friend. They make air holes in the soil so that water can get into it. That makes the soil better because the worm bodies fertilize it so you can plant better and things grow better.

Teacher's response:

Hi Debbie. I appreciate your paper about the importance of worms for enriching the soil. You also gave two examples for how the worms do this—that is, by making air holes and by the earthworm wastes that act as natural fertilizer. Can you give some examples of other natural fertilizers that can be used to enrich the soil?

> Response analysis:
>
> The teacher appreciates Debbie's work and points to two examples that she gave to support her argument. She subtly indicates that it is earthworm waste that is the natural fertilizer. She also extends Debbie's thinking by asking her for additional examples of natural fertilizers.

8. Noah, Grade 12 (law)

The case of Garufi v. School Board of Hillsborough County was tried in Florida n 1993. Mrs. Garufi, the plaintiff, was visiting Ben Hill Junior High School to collect school work for her son, Nicholas, who was recovering from injury. While walking down a corridor, she was attacked, suddenly and without provocation, by a 16-year old student, Ronald Green. Resultingly, Mrs. Garufi suffered serious injury and incurred significant medical expenses.

Following the incident, the Garufi family sued the Hillsborough County School Board for negligence. Due to the prior extensive disciplinary history of the student, the Plaintiff argues that the Defense did not take proper precautions to ensure an incident, such as this one, would not happen. Furthermore, it is the responsibility of the school administrators to protect visitors from harm. However, the Defense argued that, despite Ronald Green's history, there was no way to predict his attack on Mrs. Garufi. Additionally, there were no grounds on which school officials were required to expel Ronald Green prior to the attack.

My conclusion is to rule in favor of the Plaintiff, agreeing that the School Board of Hillsborough County was negligent. A school must take proper precautions to ensure the safety of its students, teachers and visitors. In this case, school officials should have taken more precaution regarding Ronald Green. By failing to do so, it allowed the potential for an attack like this to occur. The Plaintiff is entitled to all medical expenses and $1000 in damages for the emotional trauma incurred because of the attack.

Teacher's response:

Hi, Noah. First let me thank you for your thoughtful analysis of the *Garufi v. School Board of Hillsborough County* case. Clearly, you have given the case some thought before you came to your conclusion that the resolution should favor the plaintiff, Mrs. Garufi, as well as compensate her for her emotional trauma. That seems to me to be a very human response to the case.

On the basis of the evidence, I am wondering how, for example, a school is able to know, in advance, which students are likely to cause harm and how that should be monitored? If, for example, Ronald Green had no history of previous aggressive behavior, would that influence your decision? What other rule of law would be applied in this case? Let me know what you think and whether you will continue to argue in favor of the plaintiff.

Response analysis:

The teacher appreciates Noah's analysis and links his conclusions to the human feelings he has for the injury Mrs. Garufi has suffered. But the teacher also asks Noah to consider the evidence, on which the law must rest—that is, the evidence of any previous behavior of Ronald's that might have indicated he needed careful supervision. The teacher is pointing out the difference in law between what is felt to be right and what the law supports for Noah's further consideration.

9. Reyna, grade 10 (science—bioethics

Question: Should we let scientists clone animals to bring human cloning a little closer?

No, but to a certain level and requirements.
Justification. Very expensive to clone your pets ($100,000 - $150,000).
  Having to spend a lot of money, when the cloning might not even work.
How will the scientist find animals to supply their research of cloning, not everyone would want to have their animal tested on.
There is no 100% that the cloning would work.
Cloning pets is not illegal, but cloning a human is.

Written Diagnostic Evaluative Feedback across the Curriculum   51

After testing on animals, scientist would have to test on humans. Which means that they would need volunteers to be tested on.
It would be very expensive to fund the research for cloning ($45,000 - $75-000).
Testing could take years, and for all we know cloning humans could be impossible.
If human cloning does happen, many scientists might not even want to clone humans because they think it's to much of a risky procedure.

Teacher's response:

Thank you Reyna for your clearly stated views on cloning animals and humans. You have listed several persuasive arguments against cloning animals that could lead to cloning humans. I wonder if you would consider the following in your thoughts about cloning animals and humans:

a. What about the ethical implications of carrying out cloning experiments on animals? Where do you stand on that?
b. What about the ethical implications of cloning humans? Where do you stand on that?
c. Who should be allowed to make these kinds of decisions? What are your views on that?

Response analysis:

The teacher appreciates Reyna's response (she is a recently arrived ELS student from Vietnam), makes no criticism about her English, but rather invites her to extend her thinking further about the ethics involved in animal experimentation and who should be involved in making such decisions.

10. Anthea, grade 10 (social studies)

Synthesis: Cinderella Man and Scrapbook
Cinderella Man example—Jim and his family lived comfortably right at the beginning of the movie before the depression hit. They had a large home, plenty of food, and didn't seem worried or stressed about their finances.
Scrapbook example—Before the Great Depression, there was a sense of prosperity and general well being (page 2) but after the stock market crashed everything fell apart.
In watching Cinderella Man and reading page 2 of the Scrapbook, I got a clear idea of how much life changed when the Great Depression hit. Before the Depression, most people lived comfortably and enjoyed much of what society had to offer, such as going out for the evening to watch movies and

attending dinner parties. During this time, there was a sense of "prosperity" in the air, and people were generally happy. However, after the stock market crash, everything changed. People lost their jobs and their homes. They then had to sell all of their possessions just to help pay the bills. Families were living in one room apartments, and often went without food or electricity for long periods of time. Children were sent away because their parents could no longer properly take care of them, leaving people in a sad, unhappy state. This was demonstrated in Cinderella Man as we saw at the beginning of the movie how Jim and his family lived in a large house with plenty of food, and did not worry over meeting their basic needs. Unfortunately, this didn't last for long and they were quickly put into a situation of despair and worry. During this time, people could no longer do the things they once enjoyed during the 20's after the stock market crash. Not only did it greatly cause a shift in the culture and attitudes of individuals in the 1930's, it also left many without any hope and instead plenty of fear for what was to come.

Teacher's response:

Dear Anthea. You have painted a poignant picture of how a middle-class family suffered during the Great Depression. You note how basic human needs were no longer able to be met and that, in some cases, children had to be sent away because their families didn't have the resources to take care of them.
What do you suppose were some emotional and psychological factors that impacted these families? In other words, how do people survive such deprivation? How do they cope? Do you have any thoughts about that?

Response analysis:

The teacher highlights the poignancy of Anthea's analysis—noting that she has some empathy with the family—and affirms some of the issues she has raised. The teacher extends her thinking by raising some further questions about the impact on families of having to live without adequate funds, as this is one theme that will be returned to in later discussions about social classes.

CONCLUSION

Evaluation is a significant feature of education. Giving feedback is not a walk in the park; it is not taken lightly or without thought. It is not a rote exercise that merely points out errors. It is a key component in the network of acts that enable student learning. That is why it is so important for teachers to take the time to give thoughtful consideration of what to write, and how to present those ideas in a helpful way, in a way that asks the student to reflect on what he or she has written and take the next steps to extend thinking or to examine errors.

From the examination of the teachers' responses above, it will become immediately apparent that different teachers will view these evaluative responses differently. Some may take issue with some of the responses, looking for different emphasis on different aspects of a student's performance. Some will want to see issues highlighted that were ignored or overlooked. The bottom line is that it doesn't really matter as long as important principles of evaluative feedback are upheld because learning is not a singular act; it occurs on a continuum, over time.

Different teachers will find "what's important" a personal or educational prerogative, and they will be guided by that sense of what message they believe necessary to send to the student. Personal knowledge of the student will further illuminate the nature of the response.

Whatever the response, the primary concern is to protect the student's sense of self, so that he or she is not diminished, defeated, or censured by the teacher's comments. What's important is that the teacher's response enables the student's further inquiry, giving him or her the threshold upon which he or she can take the next steps. What's important is that the evaluative feedback be an honest expression of the teacher's sense of "right and wrong" and of what is important to address.

Some teachers will be put off by the length of some of the teachers' responses in the examples, and yes, that is an issue. But the good news is that not every piece of students' work has to be evaluated and that should, in some small way, ease the burden of written commentary.

Keep in mind that as "all roads lead to Rome," the essential purpose of evaluation is to shift the onus to the student, thereby promoting his and her own self-awareness into that act. That is one of the great gifts that teachers can give—that learners be encouraged, aided, and abetted to become their own nonbiased and nondefensive arbiters of their own work.

Chapter 6

It's All About How You Say It

Not all evaluative feedback comes in written form, although that is the basis for much of a teacher's work in assessment. Some feedback comes orally, in a classroom discussion, or in question-and-answer sessions. While the previous chapters address teachers' written feedback on students' written work, this chapter examines the nature of teachers' oral feedback to students in classroom discussions.

While the principles underlying feedback cited in the earlier chapters remain significant, an important feature of oral feedback is for the teacher to develop the ability to listen to self in the act of delivering that feedback, so that at all times the teacher is mindful of what is coming out of one's mouth. A second feature is for teachers to lose the habit of evaluating every remark a student makes, a habit that is ill-formed and counterproductive.

Although it has been assumed that students need positive affirmation to encourage their participation, judgmental responses may actually be self-defeating, cutting off further discussion, rather than facilitating it (Kohn, 1999). Once students have learned that what they say is going to be judged, this will effectively muzzle those unsure of venturing an idea, or those who fear that what they say will be wrong. Thus, some of the most original, more innovative ideas may be lost.

Alas, those more facilitative discussion skills are not learned in any education course; neither are they skills that we are born with.

REFLECTING IN ACTION

Learning to watch and listen to oneself in the act of conducting a classroom discussion is a learned skill. It is comparable to learning to listen to oneself practicing any musical instrument, tuning into the wrong notes, the cadences, the nuances, the shading, the phrasing, the smoothness of the melodic line, the quality of the sound being produced. Without such reflection in action there is little hope of attaining mastery. Learning to listen to oneself is the key to eventual success. From listening, and from discerning the effects of what has been said on students, one learns about what one has done well and what needs modification. One learns to build these "edits" in subsequent discussions. Such a cumulative process moves one toward improved skill and eventual competence (Wassermann, 2017).

Unfortunately, there is no shortcut to competence. In fact, it is a process without end, unlike learning some finite skill like mastering the multiplication tables. It is more like learning to play the Bach Preludes and Fugues. One never stops learning them.

Rather than being put off by such an admonition, it energizes many teachers as they recognize that this kind of continual professional development promises greater rewards for teachers and students. It is the kind of learning that enriches teachers as professionals and gives each classroom discussion an exciting frisson.

One of the more challenging stumbling blocks in this process is a teacher's natural inclination to use defensiveness as a shield against such critical self-examination. Learning to reflect in action involves dropping that defensiveness, being more open to one's own experience, one's own behavior. No one said that was easy.

How does that development of skill occur? Again, using learning to play an instrument as a metaphor, it is a matter of listening to oneself in the act of carrying on a classroom discussion. There are now sophisticated and easy-to-use devices that enable such self-examination.

For example, most mobile phones have built in recording devices (e.g., iPhones and Androids). Some may require downloading recording apps, which are easy to access. In fact, the Apple app store lists many paid and free options for voice recording. And in this high-tech world in which we live, some of these "smart" apps will transcribe the recording, a feature that enables a teacher to have a written transcript to study after the discussion is concluded. Spiffy!

Using self-recording, and playing the classroom discussion back, as well as examining a transcript, reveals not only the hard reality of the teacher's interactions but provides full disclosure of the teacher-to-student-to-teacher exchanges. Most important, it gives teachers hard data to use in making the necessary modifications in their future discussion-teaching modus operandi.

Another strategy is for two teachers to create a "collaborative professional partnership" in which each "monitors" the other while observing classroom discussions, feeding back to each other after the discussions to point out what the teacher was saying, how it was being said, and making suggestions for improvement. Finding a colleague with whom one has a trusting and collegial relationship, who also wants to engage in such professional development, is one alternative to self-recording.

Finally, for the truly intrepid teacher, there is the option of self-video—watching as well as listening to oneself in action. Once again, the IT world offers several options, including the use of a mobile phone that comes with a camera application built into the operating system that is capable of recording full motion video with sound.

Alas, there is no shortcut to the use of such strategies in mastering the art of leading a productive discussion that avoids judgment, and uses, instead, other discussion skills that promote and encourage student thinking and the examination of their ideas. But this can be promised: the first times are the hardest; eventually it gets easier. What makes it worthwhile is a teacher's critical observations of his and her growing competence in the art of discussion leadership and how those skills bear on the nature and consequence of classroom discussions.

But as very first steps, concentrating on losing the habit of responding with "Good!" or "That's interesting" is a promising beginning. As a quick fix, try instead: "I see." Or, perhaps, "Tell me more."

EXAMINING CLASSROOM DISCUSSIONS

As a starting point in studying and understanding more productive classroom discussions that avoid judgment, some sample transcripts of discussions are offered below.

Transcript A: Grade 3, Science Lesson about Garbage

Teacher: You were out on the playground this afternoon just after lunchtime making observations of the condition of the playground. Some of you took notes and others made some illustrations. When you came back into the classroom, some of you said that litter and trash on the playground was disgusting and suggested that the principal should take some action. What ideas do you have about that?

Heather: I think what might be a good idea is if the principal has an extra recess or something and called everybody out and everybody would have to pick up some kind of litter.

Teacher: You think the principal should get the students out to the playground and get them to participate in picking up the litter. (*Reflects student's statement*)

Heather: Uh huh.

Ray: I think they should just not let them have the privilege of having more recess or make them go home for lunch if they just drop their litter around everywhere.

Teacher: You think the principal should punish the students who drop their litter on the ground by taking away their recess and making them go home for lunch. (*Teacher reflects student's statement*)

Ray: Yeh.

Teacher: Giving students an extra recess is more like a reward which they don't deserve. (*Interprets student's idea*)

Ray: Uh huh.

Claudia: Or you could do what they did at our other school. There's four classes and each class is responsible for a different part of the school grounds. Whoever picks up the most litter gets points for their class.

Teacher: There might be a competition and the students would win points for their class. (*Teacher reflects student's idea*)

Claudia: Yeah, because they might do that because they want to get a lot more points for their class.

Teacher: It's a good idea for pupils to clean up the litter in order to win points. (*Asks student if this is a good idea.*)

Claudia: Uh huh.

Teacher: You like that way of doing it? (*Asks students to affirm her idea.*)

Claudia: Uh huh.

David: Not have an extra recess to do it—pick up all the litter. They should go out for lunch and have fun and play around but instead of doing that, have them pick up their litter at lunch.

Teacher: I'm not sure I understand your idea, David. Can you help me? Are you saying that they should not have their lunch period but would instead have a period to pick up the litter?

(*Asks student for clarification and more information*)

David: No. Well, there's forty-five minutes for lunch and they should just have part of that time to pick up the litter. Everybody would have to pick up a certain amount. I don't think they should get an extra recess for that.

Teacher: So what you are saying is that there should be some penalties involved for people who leave their litter around. You don't like the idea of giving them an extra recess. (*Interprets what student is saying*)

David: Yeh.

Teacher: I see. Thank you, David. (*Accepts nonjudgmentally*) Here's another question. Why do you suppose students leave their trash on the playground?

Colin: 'Cause they're too lazy to put it in the trash can or they just can't find one, so they throw it on the school grounds.

Teacher: You think it's a question of laziness. (*Reflects student's idea*)

Colin: Uh huh.

Claudia: Or, like, say they're playing with their friends or playing on the swing but if they get off the swing, somebody else will get on the swing so they just throw it any old place so they can keep the swing.

Teacher: You seem to be supporting what Colin is saying, Claudia, that it's a matter of laziness or being too busy. They just don't want to stop their playing to take their litter to the trash bin or lose their place on the swing. (*Interprets student's idea*)

Claudia: Uh huh.

Heather: I think sometimes it's a matter of what they think is more important. Like it's more important for me to play with my friends than go and put the litter in the garbage.

Teacher: It's a question of priorities, Heather—what you see as more important and it's more important for you to play with your friends. You would do that first rather than take your litter to the trash bin. (*Misinterprets student's statement*)

Heather: No, that's not what I'd do, but that's what some kids do.

Teacher: Some kids do that. But you wouldn't do that. You'd take the litter to the trash bin first, then play with your friends next. (*Reflects student's statement*)

Heather: Most of the time.

Teacher: Where did you get those ideas from, Heather? Can you tell us about it? (*Asks where the student's beliefs came from*)

Heather: Because when we went to Disneyland, somebody drops something on the ground and somebody picks it up and I was thinking, why should somebody do that for you when you could do it yourself?

Teacher: In other words, when you were in Disneyland, and you saw somebody picking up after the crowds of people, it made you stop and think, "Why do people behave that way?" (*Reflects student's statement*)

Heather: Yes. It was just what I felt when I went to Disneyland.

Teacher: And that helped you form some opinions that you now have about littering. (*Asks student to affirm the statement*)

Heather: Uh huh. And some of the commercials. Like that commercial when the Indian sees somebody throw their garbage out of the car window.

Teacher: I don't know that one, Heather. Would you tell me about it? (*Asks for more information*)

Heather: Well, there's this Indian and he's walking by the road and then this lady drives by in her car and she throws a bunch of garbage down and it lands right by his feet.

Teacher: I see. (*Accepts nonjudgmentally*)

Heather: And what I thought was, what he was thinking about. When they lived there, there was no litter and they kept it pretty clean. And I was just thinking about what had happened.

Teacher: Are you saying that when the white settlers took over this land from the Indians, they made some changes that the Indians would not have approved of? Like being not concerned about the protection of the environment? (*Interprets student's statement*)

Heather: Yeah.

Teacher: I see. Thank you for sharing your ideas, Heather. Does anyone want to say anything more? (*Accepts student's idea nonjudgmentally, thanks her, and invites additional discussion*)[1]

As seen in the above transcript of a grade 3 discussion on littering as part of the teacher's science program, there is an absence of judgment throughout the teacher's responses. It is a demonstration of how a teacher's use of reflective and interpretive responses, plus her shown appreciation for the students' participation promote deeper discussion about the issues.

Transcript B: Grade 6, Social Studies— Ancient Egypt—The Pyramids

Big ideas on which this unit was based: Some all-powerful leaders demand great monuments to honor and immortalize them.

Teacher: You've spent a few weeks now studying the culture, the people and the ways of life in Ancient Egypt. One of the things that intrigued you was the building of the pyramids. Who would like to begin the discussion?
Walter: I was stumped when I got a better idea of the size of them. They are enormous.
Teacher: It was their size—so huge—that puzzled you. You might have been wondering how, in those ancient times, without the use of modern machinery, they were able to build those structures. (*Reflects student's idea and extends student's thinking*)
Walter: Yeah. That was a mystery to me. But in my reading, I found that they used hundreds of slaves to do that job.
Teacher: It was their use of slaves that made it possible.
Walter: Yeah.
Tommy: They needed to have some engineers who designed them. They just couldn't be built without a design.
Teacher: A structure like that needed a design. You may be wondering who had the smarts to be able to design them. (*Reflects student's idea and interprets his statement*)
Maggie: You know, we believe that in those ancient days, people were pretty stupid. They had no modern resources, and they had no modern equipment and they had no modern schools or technology. But look at what they did. They must have had some smarts.

---

[1] Extracted from Selma Wassermann and J. W. George Ivany, 1996. *The New Teaching Elementary Science: Who's Afraid of Spiders?* 2nd edition. By permission of the publisher. New York: Teachers College, Columbia University. All rights reserved.

Teacher: We tend to assume that in those ancient days, they didn't have the knowledge or the skills to do much but look at what they produced in the pyramids. (*Reflects student's ideas*)
Maggie: Yeah. They are wonders.
Teacher: So what did they build them for? What are your ideas about that? (*Opens up a new and related question*)
Priscilla: They were tombs. They built them as tombs for the pharaohs.
Teacher: The rulers of ancient Egypt wanted them built as monuments to themselves. (*Interprets and extends her thinking*)
Priscilla: It's incredible. The pharaohs wanted to show how important they were even in death. So they had all these slaves build monuments that would be their graves.
Teacher: I'm going to suggest an idea that your statement brings to my mind. I'm getting the impression that you don't agree with a ruler's need to have such a monument built to himself.
(*Interprets student's underlying meaning*)
Priscilla: I think it's gross. I can't imagine the life of those slaves who had to work to build those monuments just to honor the pharaoh. He was that full of himself that he needed a pyramid for a tomb.
Teacher: You not only oppose such a structure, you are a little angry that a man needed to have such a monument built to honor him. (*Reflects and interprets*)
Priscilla: Yeah.
Teacher: I'm wondering if there are similar monuments built in modern times to honor people who have made a significant contribution to our lives and how such monuments serve the people of a society? (*Opens up a new line of inquiry about the use of monuments*)

Once again, Transcript B provides evidence that a thoughtful and careful discussion centered on the big ideas is carried out in the absence of teacher's judgmental responses. There is growing evidence that absence of judgment is a strong motivation for student engagement and that a highly judgmental series of responses actually diminish and curtail such engagement (Adam, 1992).

Transcript C: Grade 12, Social Studies—Elections

The grade 12 students had studied the case, "The Cranberry Orange Muffin Vote" (Bickerton et al., 1991), a microcosm of decision-making in a leadership convention, where delegates were assembled to elect the new head of British Columbia's Social Credit Party. The big ideas that the teacher wanted students to examine were: how voters make decisions about whom to vote for is dependent on a variety of factors, not all of them rational; and voters are vulnerable to a variety of pressures from different sources, and different groups use different means to win voters' confidence and support.

Teacher: You've read the case, *The Cranberry Orange Muffin Vote*, and I'd like to ask you what your impressions are about how voters choose the best candidate?

Megan: Well, I think the media influences our views. Also we like to use the newspapers and the TV stations that support our own preferences.

Teacher: So newspapers and TV programs are strong influences. And you're saying that people listen to programs and read newspapers that are already in line with their own thinking. *(Reflects student's idea)*

Megan: Yeh. We don't open our minds to other opinions. We know what we know.

Teacher: Some of us close our minds to different opinions. *(Reflects student's idea)*

Megan: Yeh. I don't think it's healthy.

Teacher: What were some influences on the delegates choices in the case you read? *(Raises a related question)*

Scott: It's not called the cranberry orange muffin case for nothing. The people trying to influence the delegates were tempting them with muffins and coffee and who knows what other foods.

Teacher: They were using food to get the delegates on their side? *(Reflects student's idea)*

Scott: You would think the delegates would be smart enough not to fall for that! Come on! You can buy my vote with a muffin!

Teacher: You seem to be a little outraged that votes can be bought so cheaply. That people are so easily influenced to give their votes away just for a muffin. *(Reflects the idea and the underlying feeling)*

Scott: You would think they'd be smart enough not to be tempted to give their vote away for a muffin.

Teacher: You seem disappointed that delegates would be bought so cheaply. *(Reflects student's idea)*

Scott: Yeah.

Teacher: Outside of using muffins and food, how do you suppose voters are influenced in elections these days? *(Uses the case as a basis for opening up the inquiry into a broader area)*

Carne: Well, like Megan said before, the TV and the newspapers try to persuade you.

Teacher: And how do they do that, Carne? Do you have some ideas about it? *(Asks for supporting data)*

Carne: There are editorials in the newspapers and there are commentators on TV that actually come out in favor of a particular candidate.

Teacher: Editorials and TV commentators are influential. *(Reflects student's idea)*

Carne: Yes, they do. And as Megan said, we like to read and listen to the ones that favor the candidate that we already favor.

Teacher: We don't open our minds to other views. We tend to stick to the media that support our choice. (*Reflects student's idea*)

Steve: I think the media plays a big role in presenting a candidate favorably. You know, how they appear on camera, what clothes they wear, whether the person is attractive, or smiles or doesn't smile. These are the factors that seem to count.

Teacher: What a person looks like, how they appear, has a lot to do with how a voter makes a choice. (*Reflects student's idea*)

Steve: I think it's sad but true. People don't listen. They don't want to hear the facts. They respond to slogans and to appearances. Like Trump, "Make America Great Again." What's that supposed to mean? But people believe that.

Teacher: You are distressed about the way voters make choices and how slogans that have little meaning are so influential. (*Reflects student's idea*)

Melanie: There's also the issue of fake news. How are listeners supposed to know the difference between good information and lies? A lot of candidates running for office lie all the time.

Teacher: Some candidates are using false information to win voters over. It's hard to know what's true. (*Teacher reflects student's idea*)

Connie: There's a lot of media hype and then the issue gets reduced to the simplest terms. Voters get emotional and don't fully understand the real issues.

Teacher: The candidates and the media are guilty of provoking the voters' passions with slogans and false information. And voters themselves vote with their passions instead of with their brains? Have I gone too far in interpreting what you have said? (*Reflects the ideas and asks if the interpretation is correct*)

As the three sample transcripts of classroom discussions show, even when a teacher refrains from offering judgments about students' responses, there is still much active discussion as well as opportunity for them to think more deeply about the big ideas of the lesson. Data suggest that not only do students think more about the big ideas, but that they also feel safer in telling what they think (Adam, 1991).

This is not to say that teachers never offer praise; sometimes a teacher will tell a student that his or her ideas are profound and add immeasurably to the discussion. Sometimes a teacher will tell a student that her story was so moving that it made the teacher weep. Sometimes a teacher will say, LaToya, I really appreciate what you have told us. Or even, Sven, I wonder if you'd like to reconsider that idea and give yourself some more time to think about it.

The important points are for teachers to maintain full control of what they are saying, so that what they had intended to say is congruent with what is coming out of their mouth. And to "tame" those judgmental responses so that they are not automatic, but come as thoughtful, well deserved responses to a singular piece of work.

When students feel safe to respond, when they are eager to offer their ideas, knowing that they will be respectfully heard and used as "working material," when student-teacher discussions are rich and reach for the nuggets of deeper understanding, then the teacher's responses are clearly bearing fruit.

HOOKED ON PRAISE

While many of us delight in hearing that our work is superb, there is a negative underside to the overuse of affirmative praise. Students are likely to get mired in the need for positive affirmation if they have learned to believe that only an outside source, like the teacher, or a parent has the power to decide what that student has done is of worth. When that occurs, that student has lost all power to appreciate, for himself or herself, the value of that piece of work or performance. The student becomes increasingly dependent on others to know that he or she is OK. There is an unhealthiness in that kind of dependency. The bad news is that teachers may be the inadvertent culprits in promoting it.

Another side of that coin is a student's reluctance to do or say anything unless there is a positive reward for that behavior; it's not the learning that is the key motivation, it's the reward. According to Kohn (1999), a child promised a treat for learning or acting responsibly has been given every reason to stop doing so when there is no longer a reward to be gained.

The danger lies in a teacher's or parent's unconscious overuse of words of affirmation when a child presents some piece of work, a statement, a solution to a problem, a perfect paper. The word "good" falls from the lips in a staccato drumbeat. In a misguided belief, it is supposed to encourage, support, give credence to our approval of the work or act. In fact, it does the opposite.

That is not to say that a teacher or parent never tells a child that what he or she has done is of value. But it is the automatic response, and the overuse, that is counterproductive. The negative effects of a student's dependency on praise are more than unhealthy. It is demeaning.

Teachers who have become more conscious of their use of positive affirmation in excess, and are trying to tame that response, may find some resistance in students who have already become habituated to it. So not only teachers need weaning; students do as well.

In such cases, it is helpful for teachers to bring students into the "know"— letting them know why the teacher is being more selective in giving positive rewards for their work, citing the reasons and acknowledging their questions and concerns. Once students are apprised of the why and the what and the how, they are more than likely to understand and respect the reasons.

Once again, the onus is on the teacher to become more aware of his and her responses, to take those pains to ensure that what is being said is entirely congruent with what has been intended.

Among the many professional tasks of teachers, this is perhaps one of the most demanding.

Chapter 7

Impediments to Good Diagnostic Judgment

The professional tasks of a teacher are wide and deep and no one who has not spent time in a classroom full of energetic, individually challenged, excitable students can fully appreciate all that a teacher does and must do every minute of every teaching day. The complexities of teaching and the arduous demands of the job are impossible to discern to anyone outside of the profession. Yes, there are good reasons that teachers are exhausted at the end of each teaching day, why they are drained each Friday afternoon, why they look to the holidays as oases that replenish body and soul.

Shedding the myth that teaching is nothing more than standing in front of a group of students day after blah blahing day, and examining the multiple and extensive facets of a teacher's functioning, it is possible to discern the true nature of what teachers do in the act of "teaching."

They are responsible for designing curriculum experiences for their students and for the preparation of original learning materials that are consistent with the goals of instruction. They are required to understand and deal effectively with the emotional, social, and intellectual needs of students and give each the individual time and attention needed in order that improved learning may result.

Teachers formatively and summatively evaluate students' learning, making diagnoses of performance on specific tasks, making thoughtful judgments about a student's performance over time, and reporting all of this in comprehensible ways to anxious parents. Teachers are called upon to work as competently with large groups as they do with small groups and individuals, even though the approach to each may require different types of skills. They must be masters of the interactive process, knowing when and how to inform and tell, when to ask, when to challenge student thinking, when to remain neutral, and when and how to offer an evaluative judgment.

A teacher must be prepared to deal with students' behavior problems, knowing when and how to be tough and firm without diminishing a student's dignity, and when to overlook the indiscretion. A teacher must know how to organize the classroom for instruction and how to make shifts in the organization so that the learning activity and the organizational scheme are in accord. The teacher must be the composer, the orchestrator, and the conductor of the classroom symphony, if the players are to make beautiful music. On top of all of that, teachers must also keep up with their professional development activities, reading what is current, attending meetings and workshops, and making intelligent distinctions about what new ideas are of real value (Wassermann, 2015).

It is no wonder that teachers are tired. The job is gargantuan, seemingly beyond human capability.

Yet, teachers are very human. They, like those in all other professions, have human needs: needs to feel successful in what they do, needs to be liked, needs to feel affirmed for their work, needs to feel safe in their workplaces, needs for recognition, needs for self-respect, to name a few. Virtually every teacher wants to be a good teacher—one who provides the kind of learning environment that enables students to grow and learn.

To be human also means to lay claim to our own flaws. And one of these is the admittance that we have biases, preferences, predilections, and, yes, prejudices. In a classroom, it may mean that we have a tendency to like and appreciate some students more than others; it may mean that we have a tendency to dislike and disapprove of some students more than others. Some of those biases emerge from the ways in which students reveal their behavior to teachers. In other words, those students who show a high interest in learning, who are well behaved, who never forget their homework, and who are attentive and never get into trouble are those for whom teachers might feel more partial.

Those students who don't pay attention, who forget their homework repeatedly, who get into fights, and who bully others are those about whom teachers may feel annoyance, disfavor, disapproval. These are utterly natural and normal responses. Teachers, who are among the most caring professionals, are not neutral. And no suggestion is being made that teachers *should* be neutral, or value-free. If we were, we'd be a bloodless, uninteresting lot.

What is being suggested, however, is that in a classroom such biases must be brought under control, never to be revealed, never to manifest in the way teachers interact with their students. Owning them is perhaps the first step in managing them, so that they never interfere with what a teacher says and how a teacher acts. And this is one more challenge in a teacher's methods and manner of evaluation. That is, a teacher's biases must not get in the way of his or her fair and honest evaluative responses to students.

TAMING THE IMPULSE TO PUNISH BY EVALUATIVE JUDGMENT

It is not an easy task for us teachers to overcome our predispositions about their students. "I'm not prejudiced," says Mr. Camrose, "but . . ." At once you know, as you listen to him in the staff room, that not only are his biases deep and far-reaching, but that he is unable to face the fact that he has them.

As Clark Moustakas recognized so many years ago, "Every child wants to be known as a unique person, yet most teachers find it difficult or impossible to respect individual differences. With so many other pressures and responsibilities, with such large groups, with prescribed curriculum requirements, the teacher's time and energies are almost completely used up . . . and better human relations are too often, ideas and dreams" (Moustakas, 1966).

Yet, as teachers move toward more self-awareness, more open to themselves and their own needs, values, and beliefs, they do become more accepting of the vagaries and foibles that each student presents.

One step in this direction is for teachers to "learn" about their students—to spend time with each individually, to learn about them from the inside out. In other words, to develop a personal as well as a professional relationship with them. For to know students better is one way to know what motivates them, what needs, values, and beliefs trigger their behaviors, and what each dreams about for himself/herself.

Teachers who treat all the students in a class as one student—expecting the same from each—will not be able easily to overcome any prejudices they hold, either favorably or not. Teachers who are able to develop strong personal relationships with a student will very likely soon be disabused of any false notions about what is going on behind the façade of the behavior.

Moustakas has written that "a teacher is sometimes afraid to confront a student who is hostile, caustic or vengeful. Such a teacher avoids and avoids until the accumulation of feelings becomes so unbearable an explosion occurs and the teacher loses control" (Moustakas, 1966). It is when those negative feelings subside that teachers are better able to sit down with the student and begin to develop a more personal relationship. The student who is hostile, angry, and perhaps even destructive can be addressed better in a one-on-one consultation, to clear out the angry feelings and move toward a more agreeable connection. Unless we meet these students head on, we can't really "learn" about them.

When teachers begin to know, to really KNOW an individual student, it becomes much easier to tame those impulses to impose heavy negative judgments. In that regard, it is helpful to remember Bobby's admonition to his teacher: Good teachers must have love, even for the bad ones.

The ability to put oneself in another's shoes is called "empathy." Since every person's behavior is an acting out of their individual needs, a teacher's ability to see the world from the student's perspective can be a helpful strategy in overcoming personal bias. Training oneself to do that, to drop any predisposition to judge, and to look at the world from the student's seat is a helpful tool in not only developing more positive relationships, but in unloading one's own prejudices.

Learning to become more empathic has a payoff even greater than overcoming one's biases. Teachers, for example, who show higher levels of empathic functioning, who are respectful of all their students, and who are genuine in their responses and in their overall behavior, can expect a large return in improved human relations in the classroom. As Carkhuff has suggested, "With such conditions present in classrooms, teachers can expect a more constructive physical, emotional and intellectual climate for growth and learning" (Carkhuff, 1969).

This is no small potatoes.

TWO CENTS WORTH OF ADVICE TO TEACHERS

Given the data above—about the heavy load that teachers carry each teaching day—here is yet one more piece of advice for the already-overburdened evaluator of students' work. When sitting down to mark or grade or give feedback on a student's paper, ask yourself, first, how you are perceiving that student, how you have judged him or her in the past, and what "baggage" you are bringing to your comments. If you discern even a trace of bias for or against, it might be a good time to walk away from the paper, have a cup of tea, look out the window at the birds building a nest, and take a walk in the park. And then return to the task with a fresh eye.

Another strategy is to begin by obscuring the names of the students, so that the author's name on the paper does not influence your judgment.

One teacher suggested writing, spontaneously, a short profile of each student in the class without editing out any thoughts. In the profile write about how you perceive the student as a group member. Several days later, read the profiles, with an eye to the kind of thinking that is seen in the profile. For example, what value judgments were made? Were they negative or positive? What labels were used? Were they negative or positive? What generalizations were made? Were they positive or negative? And in summary, what biases were revealed in the profile?

Such strategies will not guarantee an evaporation of all biases. They may, however, help in promoting teachers' own awareness of their existence and provide some beginning tools in their management.

None of the above precludes teachers inventing their own strategies. The point of the exercise is to recognize one's personal biases and develop some steps that enable one to overcome them.

For when biases are allowed to infiltrate evaluative judgment, all pretense of honesty and fairness is lost.

Chapter 8

Reporting to Parents

One of the important purposes of evaluation is to provide feedback to parents about their child's progress and growth. Every concerned parent wants to know: How's my child doing? This encompasses considerably more than academic performance.

Communicating to parents on a regular and ongoing basis allows both learners and parents to evaluate where the students "are" in relation to the grade or subject standards, what they are working toward, and the ways in which their learning is supported. In this way, both students and parents are provided with meaningful information or feedback about their learning, so that they can monitor their progress toward the learning goals of the grade/subject.

At Charles Dickens Primary School, guidelines for formal written reports to parents indicate the student's "position" on articulated levels of performance. For example:

- He/she is BEGINNING to acquire knowledge, skills, strategies, and processes
- He/she is DEVELOPING the ability to apply knowledge, skills, strategies, and processes
- He/she is APPLYING knowledge, skills, strategies, and processes consistently
- He/she is EXTENDING knowledge, skills, strategies, and processes creatively and strategically

Feedback on these standards of performance enables parents to become partners in a dialogue about their child's progress with an eye toward how they may support them as learners.

Of course, no parent wants bad news; most of them are hoping to learn that their offspring excels, is better than, has great competence in, and so on and so forth. Something to take home and rejoice in. Keeping that in mind, teachers will want to temper any "bad news" with kindness and emphasize the good over the bad, without crossing the line into dishonesty and flagrant abuse of the truth.

Nevertheless, parents need to know what areas the teacher perceives in which more work is needed, bringing that to the attention of parents who may wish to keep track of how they might contribute to the promotion of those skills and attitudes at home.

In many schools, reporting to parents includes different methods of communication within a school year. Parent-teacher conferences are normally scheduled several times a year (or semester); interim written reports may go out several times as well; a summative report is usually sent at the end of the year.

Many schools, especially in the primary years, now refrain from issuing letter grades—and those that disdain them may offer them to parents on request.

EXAMPLES OF WRITTEN REPORTS TO PARENTS

Given the fact that concerned parents will want to know "how my child is doing?" such a question demands a more comprehensive and detailed account, for nothing less can satisfy a parent's right to know. Once again, the standards for a subject or grade will inform what the teacher can say to illuminate a student's classroom performance. Teachers who write written reports to parents have the advantage of being able to sit down and think, mulling over what to write and how to present the ideas clearly, which is, perhaps, easier than giving information in a parent-teacher conference. Avoiding such educational jargon as "he's working up to his potential," reports can be more specifically focused.

Parents who receive evaluative feedback, either in written or oral form, that speaks clearly about their child's strengths and areas of needed development and does so respectfully and with full caring about the student in evidence, will be satisfied to have a greater understanding and appreciation of how their child is doing in the classroom. Knowing, also, that the teacher understands and is making "best efforts" to help the student improve in those areas where he or she needs help will be of great reassurance.

Some examples of teachers' written reports:

a. Max, grade 4—end-of-term report

   Max is an active, happy and eager participant in the fourth grade. He is hard working and motivated in class. In math, Max exhibits a positive attitude. He has good organizational skills and is very concerned with the quality and neatness of his work. Max learns best when using math manipulatives to help him understand the concept being taught. This concrete way of learning helps to develop his confidence so that he can move onto more abstract ways of thinking. Repetition and practice seem to help Max retain new skills.

   In science, Max is attentive and participates in class. He seems to especially enjoy class projects and experiments. I applaud his efforts and his contributions.

b. Allan, grade 3—midterm report

   Allan is an eager and involved member of our Reading Lab. He usually works well with others and is able to follow directions and work independently on assignments as well.

   Allan's reading skills are progressing nicely. Orally, he reads with more fluency and better expression. We are working on developing silent reading skills and responding to text both orally and in writing. Allan writes accurate and thoughtful responses to literature. He needs to work on using proper pronunciation and capitalization and larger print.

c. Susan, grade 4—end-of-term report

   Susan is an interested and motivated learner. She volunteers more now in discussions and contributes meaningfully. She asks great questions that are truly geared for specific knowledge. Susan will stick with something for a long time if she is enjoying the challenge and task at hand. She sometimes sets unrealistic goals for herself and feels badly if she does not meet them in an appropriate amount of time. Susan still needs to gain more confidence in her abilities to really perform at optimal level.

   Susan's self-esteem in relation to her peers has improved a great deal. Her friendships are becoming stronger and she is reaching out to more people. She has good insight about people and shows an awareness of their feelings. In general, she has good work habits and is able to handle her routines well. She is a good role model to her peers and is very helpful to them. We enjoy her great sense of humor, imagination and creativity. We will continue to work on organization skills and attention to neatness and presentation.

d. Freddy, grade 1—end-of-term report

   As you know, we have been working on Freddy's small motor skills, and he has shown a lot of improvement in being able to manipulate his pencils *to form letters and write words that are more clearly readable. He is able to give more attention to his seatwork and has no longer such a great need to be moving around. His speech is improving, and he can make himself more clearly understood.*

We've been using word cards to help him focus and remember basic vocabulary. His sense of the sounds of letters still needs work and perhaps this is something you can work on with him over the summer months. He is a very sweet boy, very affectionate and seems happy to be with his classmates. He is well liked by his classmates and it has been a great pleasure to work with him this year.

e. Judy, grade 6—midterm report

As you know we have been concentrating on building students' thinking skills, a focus of our work this year that has been integrated into subject area learning. Judy began with some resistance to doing her own thinking, and this was manifest in her repeated asking for help. Slowly she began to move toward greater independence and is now at the point where she enjoys doing things for herself. This is a major gain for her. She now seems unafraid to offer her ideas and doesn't have to preface her contributions with a qualifier or disclaimer. Her work on group projects is creative. When she speaks in class, she has good ideas to contribute and what she says makes sense. I see a huge improvement in her work and behavior in these last few months.

f. Michael, grade 5—midterm report

Michael has had some behavior issues that have gotten in the way of his ability to do his work. There is no question in my mind that he is capable and has the intelligence to do well. His need to act out, however, is a big impediment to his intellectual functioning. I am sad to report that he has not shown a lot of progress in his academic skills, but I am confident that with your support at home, he may be helped to overcome these behaviors and settle down to learning.

g. Laura, grade 11 (social studies)—end-of-year report

Laura has done exceptionally fine work in our social studies class. She has made significant and thoughtful contributions to class discussions and the quality of her thinking on her assignments is superior. She is a careful and thoughtful group member and not only are her contributions of merit, but she also addresses the thinking of others, pointing out where discrepancies lie and how they might reconsider their ideas.

She is respectful and tolerant of the ideas of others, and when she offers her own suggestions to others, they are offered in helpful and never critical ways. The work she did on the end-of-term project was clearly outstanding—showing originality and great creativity. I am proud to have been her teacher.

h. Malcolm, grade 10—(social studies)—midterm assessment

Malcolm is a frequent contributor to class and group discussions and has vigorous points of view. He enjoys presenting his ideas and he seems to have a need for others to appreciate what he has to say. In fact, he has a very strong presence in the classroom and I think it would be safe to say he enjoys the work we have been doing. The areas where he needs some attention lie in his certainty about issues where he needs to be more circumspect. In short, he argues without sufficient basis in correct information, most from his own opinions rather than from the data.

We have been working hard to help him to develop his higher order thinking skills as I believe this would be a great asset in helping him overcome his dogmatism. He seems a willing and eager participant in this work and that is a huge positive factor.

i. Maya, grade 3—end-of-term report

Maya has been a wonderful child to teach! I have enjoyed having her in my class. She is a wonderful reader—reads aloud fluently and enjoys reading to herself. She has probably read about thirty books this year! Her work in math has been consistently good; she understands number concepts and does her computation without major errors. She has shown great creativity in her original writing and poems and seems to enjoy doing that a great deal. She is well liked by the other children and enjoys playing with them. She is not a risk taker and prefers to work on the safe side, which is not a problem! She is open to new ideas and new suggestions and she happily participates in new projects. I predict a very happy and productive year for her in grade 4. She is a pleasure to teach.

j. Fumiko, grade 11 (English)—end-of-term report

Fumiko is one of the most outstanding students in my class. Her writing skills are superb, and she has one of the most creative and original minds I have seen! In fact, I have suggested to her that she submit some of her stories to journals that publish student work. In her written work, she is able to go beyond the ordinary and create new ideas, new images and new inventions. Her use of metaphor and imagery are well beyond the levels of most grade 12 students. In her writing and in sharing her ideas in classroom discussions, she is able to take cognitive risks and she pushes herself to the limits of creativity.

I feel confident in suggesting that she has a bright future ahead of her as a writer of some distinction.

k. Craig, grade 8—midterm report

As we have discussed in the past, Craig has been experiencing a lot of difficulty with some of the challenges in grade 8. He is overly timid about tackling new problems, and his first response is, "I can't do this." I am attributing this to his lack of confidence in himself—as I believe that he does have the intelligence and the skills to work well. It's his belief in himself that seems to be defeating him from trying.

I'm wondering how we can, together, work with him and try to help him overcome his lack of confidence in himself.

1. Julie, grade 10 (science)—end-of-term report

As you already know, our grade 10 science program has concentrated on students' ability to use science concepts learned in class to the application of that knowledge in self-selected projects and investigations. This project work subsumes several analytical skills, such as being able to frame problems, collecting and organizing data, the analysis of assumptions, and the generation of hypotheses. Evidence of all those higher order mental functions is seen in the way the students demonstrate that in their project designs. Julie has shown exceptional skill in all of these areas. She seems to have a real interest and passion for science and I believe her work this term has been of the highest caliber.

PARENT-TEACHER AND PARENT-STUDENT-TEACHER CONFERENCES

The parent-teacher conference is a highly individualized and personal tool for evaluation of student learning. The conference may involve examination of a broad range of skills, or focus on selected skills, depending on what the teacher believes is more appropriate for that particular time and that particular setting. As in most situations where reporting to parents or to students is an issue, having a clear idea of what the goals and standards are for a subject or grade is the template on which the evaluative messages are based.

In many schools, students are also participants in these evaluative conferences. And where this is done, teachers and parents have noted that the students themselves add an important dimension to what is being discussed and how the assessment is being made. In other words, student participation in these conferences is additive. Where this is practiced, students are involved in giving their own views of how well they have met the grade standards and what they perceive to be areas of great need for further study.

Whether the students participate or not, it is a good idea for teachers (and students) to have examples of student work to be presented to parents to give additional credence to the assessment. Parents may be asked to comment, either directly to the student or to the teacher, in response to their view of the student's work. Teachers' roles in these conferences may be both evaluative and facilitative.

When students are part of the parent-teacher conference, they may prepare by focusing their thoughts on some of the following questions:

A. What do you consider to be your most significant learning this semester with respect to:
   a. understanding the issues that have been examined in the course
   b. working in groups
   c. participating in class discussions
   d. evaluating your own work
B. Is there an area requiring your most urgent attention? How do you plan to deal with this? (Adam, 1991)

While the above suggestions seem more applicable to older students (middle grades, secondary), it has been the experience of many teachers that even children in the primary years can be important and helpful contributors to parent-teacher conferences. The preparation the students do prior to these conferences is considered an important part of their learning process.

Cheryl MacDonald (1982), a primary grade teacher from British Columbia, might have been among the first to promote the involvement of her primary grade students in parent conferences. Her written report of that experience was published in the provincial teachers' journal, and it suggested that not only the problems of logistics, for example, the scheduling, were easily solved. She found, too, enthusiastic support for this practice from parents, who were impressed with their children's abilities to participate in such self-evaluation.

In MacDonald's program, the children personally invited their own parents to come to school at a prescheduled time, and each child ushered his or her own parents to the classroom. Once there, the child and parents viewed a videotape of the class in action, observing how the child interacted and worked in the classroom setting. The parents also looked at photographs that showed the children engaged in various activities throughout the school year.

The child then showed the parents around the classroom, pointing out the work he or she had done at school. The child might also teach the parents some of the things he or she had learned. After these introductory activities, children shared with their parents a report they had written describing perceived strengths and/or weaknesses in each subject area and personal goals for the rest of the year. The student's self-report followed an open-ended format for each curriculum area, similar to the examples given earlier. In each area, important learning activities were listed for the child to comment on.

The teacher then shared the report she had written about the child's observed strengths and areas of needed improvement. The teacher had already shown this to the child, so there were no surprises.

How did children respond to their involvement in these evaluative conferences? Some of the following (unedited) indicate that not only do even very young children know about themselves, but they can write with astonishing frankness and perception. Allowing for this self-awareness to grow, uncorrupted by the need to impress others for good marks, is an important key to a child's empowerment.

I think I am a good reader, but I just need to practice a little to get faster.
My goal on reading is to be a very good reader by the end of spring break.
I am a good reader because I read smoothly. I am a bookworm.
I think I am a good listener because I get lots of things right.
I am improving buy consontrating.
I'm not good for printing but I do my best.
Most of the children are better printers than I am, but I have improved since September.
I print beautifully But sometimes when I'm mad I don't print very good.
I have no trouble with my speaking, but sometimes I forget what I'm going to say.
I am good at doing arithmetic. I can borrow and carry now. I know how to tell time and factoring.
I am slow on substraction and speed drills and carrying. I am fast on 1,2,3, 5 and 10x. I am fast on fractions.
I work by myself and don't look at other people's books. I am nice to friends. I never hurt other people's feelings and whenever anyone wants help I tell them how to figure it out.
I think if I'm a little bit kinder I will have more friends. (MacDonald, 1982)

What was once an innovative addition to parent-teacher conferences, MacDonald's pioneering work in 1982 has now become common practice in Canada. When a father was asked if his eight-year-old daughter participated in parent-teacher conferences at the Qualicum Beach Elementary School, he said, quite proudly, "She LEADS the conference!" According to Cromwell (2015), student-led conferences in the United States is now a "growing trend." Not only do students agree that this is a worthwhile endeavor, the data from parents suggest, as well, that their experience with student-led conferences is overwhelmingly positive.

For those teachers who want to learn more about how to conduct them and what preparations are necessary to get the most of the experience, Cromwell suggests the following readings:

Kinney, Patti, Munroe, Mary Beth, Sessions, Pam. 2000. *A School Wide Approach to Student-Led Conferences: A Practitioners Guide*, published by the National Middle School Association; Piciotto, Linda-Pierce. 1997. *Student-Led Parent Conferences*, published by Scholastic.

Benson, Barbara and Barnett, Susan. 2005. *Student-Led Conferencing Using Showcase Portfolios*. Published by Corwin Press, Inc.

One of the golden rules of education is never to underestimate children. Their thoughtfulness, frankness, and sensibility are a model for us adults as they come to terms with how they see themselves as learners and people. Their involvement in parent-teacher evaluative conferences is more than additive; it is a gift.

Chapter 9

Students as Self-Evaluators

The students in the grade 6 class at the Lee Road Elementary School in New York were entirely new to the process of self-evaluation. In fact, if truth be told, at the very first, their cries of protest suggested that they believed that evaluation was the teacher's job and perhaps the teacher might have been shirking her responsibilities in transferring the burden of evaluation to them. Students are socialized by their school experiences and consequently believe that what has been done before is not only written in stone but reality.

The teacher, however, was committed to the idea that the engagement of students in a self-evaluative process was an important and perhaps vital dimension of their learning and of their empowerment. So, despite their complaints and their accusations, she proceeded, at first, to orient them to the procedures as well as to the rationale for their engagement in the process, outlining the procedures, and making clear the how and the what.

Self-evaluation reports became a part of their weekly and monthly activities. These included more than asking for their self-assessments in subject areas. They included tasks that called for growing self-awareness in a variety of personal and group activities. The more they developed these insights, the greater their awareness grew. By the end of the school year, each had grown immeasurably in his and her ability to make fair, thoughtful, and perceptive assessments of their work, their interactions with others and their overall behavior. By the end of the year, the sum of all of their previous experiences in self-awareness activities more than prepared them for writing their own report cards.

I want to learn because . . . Well let's put it this way. I have to learn if I want to be an architect (and that's what I want). I like to learn sertain [sic] *subjects and others (ugh) I don't like. I like language because of themes, but then again I don't like spelling because it drives me nuts with all the words. And then theys* [sic] *subjects I only like half and half like arithmetic. I like to* learn how to do a problem, but certain exxamples [sic] drive me battey [sic]. I like most of the subjects and what you have to know to do it, but others are out of orbit. I like to learn and I have to learn, so I can't fight, can I?

I think I'm tall and long I think I'm a normal thinker, what I mean is, I'm not dumb and I'm not brilliant. I am a good drawer sometimes, but there are days when I can't draw a straight line. I think Im good in social studies and off and on in science (it all depends on the subject), but in spelling, oh brother! I like most sports and enter most events, but there are times I can't even kick a ball. I like hobbies such as putting together models and collecting odds and ends which my mother calls junk! I like to read about famous generals of the past and wars and countries.

I like school for one reason. I learn there and the other is if there were no school I wouldn't have anything to do and I would soon get bored. I like to travel and I've gone to a lot of places in the country. I like animals and once in awhile I find an animal I like in the woods or the pet store (but that's very rare that I get one). I like my friends (that's because I've been playing with them for ten years) and go to many places with them. I like many things, but best of all I like my parents and brothers.

I want to learn because I want to be a person who knows things. If I didn't want to learn when I grow up I would be a bum. When I grow up I want to be a lawyer. To be a lawyer takes a lot of hard work. I will have to go to college and law school. When I get out of school I will be all by myself. I will also have to have a personality. That's why I want to learn.

All and all I think I am a good boy. Because I don't make wise cracks around people. Also I don't hang around with the big shots of my age who think they are big smoking, stealing, etc. Also I think I would not be liked by anyone if I was a big shot. Personally I think I should give credit to my parents for this. They help a lot by telling me right from wrong, telling me what things I do good and what I do bad, and how to improve the bad things. My parents do this because they know that some day I am going to be a man and live a hard life. I think my parents should get all the credit for my behavior and deserve all of God's will.

All and all I have had a good year in self-disciplining myself. I say I improved because I am on my own this year. Last year every day this was the plan made by my teacher in the morning: Math, 9:00–10:00; Reading 10:00–11:00; Talk 11:00–12:00. But now I can do work whenever I want to in the morning and I think I have done very well. But also I have some failures as every human person. Some of them are some days not following my plans, fooling around etc. But I have had a good year.

Reading, I think that it goes okay. But I am only a failure in science and social studies, because I don't like them. I am successful (I think) in math. Why do I feel this way? My mind tells me. My mind only goes wrong when I don't know anything or I am sick.

I think I learned a lot. I like the independent program. I found that in math I learned that if I want to learn math I can learn math, but if I don't want to that [sic] there's nothing I must do. I plan my day. I plan the days the way I want, and if I want a conference in reading I ask the teacher and if she says yes, I do so. But I very much like the independent program. I like it because of planning my own day and the conference and also the freedom I have.

I think that I could do much better work in spelling if I get into the happit [sic] of doint [sic] it. I would like to but I can't get into the happit [sic]. In math I can do OK. In reading if I get the book that I like I can read for a long time and if it is quiet. In social studies I like the way we are doing it in diffent [sic] groups. Science I do like the way we are doing that to [sic] but I would like to study airplanes.

At the end of the school year, final report cards with letter grades were required to be sent to parents. To prepare the students for this, the teacher made a "clone" of a report card and duplicated copies for each of the students. She explained the notation system and gave each student a copy to be filled out. The process involved first, students completing the cards for themselves; second, a conference with the teacher so that each could explain his or her reasons for assigning themselves that grade; and third, the teacher's transfer of the students' self-assessments onto the regular cards.

There were only two instances during the student-teacher conferences in which the teacher queried the student's assessment. One was the grade Harold gave himself for math, which seemed to the teacher to have been an overestimation of what he had accomplished. She asked him to give his rationale for the grade, given that he had not completed a great deal of his math work. He told her that it was important that he took home a grade of B for math, for if he didn't, his father would murder him. The teacher allowed Harold's grade to stand.

In the second case, Margaret seemed to have devalued her work in each of the subject areas, giving herself lower grades than the teacher thought reflected her performance. When the teacher queried Margaret about that, she demurred; she thought that giving herself higher grades would be an example of arrogance. In this case, the teacher asked Margaret to reconsider and reevaluate herself based not on her humility, but on her assessment of how well she had done on her work.

CHILDREN EVALUATING THEMSELVES IN THE PRIMARY GRADES: THE CHILD IN THE PROCESS

As the teacher in the grade 6 classroom prepared the students for their final self-assessment on the district report cards, so do many primary teachers prepare their students for more summative evaluative reports. Since self-evaluation is a learned skill, a good beginning is to engage students in teacher-student conferences in which issues of self-assessment are discussed.

In conferences with children, the teacher asks, in respectful and nonjudgmental ways, that the child make an assessment of his or her work. The questions the teacher asks address those aspects of interactive or performance behavior that the teacher considers important. As the child engages in self-assessment, the teacher never betrays the child by disagreeing or agreeing.

This is not an adversarial relationship, nor is it a game to guess what the teacher thinks.

As the child offers his or her views, the teacher paraphrases or interprets, requiring the child to reflect on his or her assessment, and then responds respectfully to what the child has said. If the teacher wants to offer data that are discrepant with what the child is saying, this, too, is offered nonjudgmentally, rather than a means of confronting the child with the error of his or her ways. The more children are asked to reflect on their own performance, the safer they feel about owning their own judgments about self, and the more they grow capable of making informed, intelligent judgments about their work.

Even very young children can be involved in self-evaluation. While they may not be very skilled at the outset, they learn to do this better with experience over time.

Some questions and invitations to respond used in conferences that help children to grow in their self-evaluative skills include the following:

- Tell me about how you worked in your group today.
- Tell me about some of the things you liked about your work.
- Tell me about some of the things that did not work well for you.
- What are some things you could do for yourself?
- What were some things you needed help with?
- When you had some trouble, tell me about how you solved the problem.
- Tell me about some of the new ideas you had.
- What did you think you did the best of all? How did you feel about that?
- Were there things you didn't try? Tell me about them.
- Which work made you feel very proud? Tell me about it.
- Tell me about how you helped with the clean up.
- Tell me what you did when you saw David crying.

An example of an evaluative conference

Teacher: Tell me about the way you worked with the plants in your group.
Marcy: We needed to decide who was going to use the magnifying glass first.
Teacher: And how did you do that?
Marcy: I told them that everybody had a turn for two minutes. I could check them with my watch.
Teacher: So you were in charge of the group work.
Marcy: Yeh. I was the boss.
Teacher: Tell me if you think this worked well for your group.
Marcy: They like for me to be the boss. To tell them what to do.
Teacher: Hm. I was wondering about that. Could you tell me, if they like it, how come they were fighting with you? I don't seem to understand that.
Marcy: They weren't fighting. They're just being silly.
Teacher: So it's okay for you to boss them around. They like it.
Marcy: Well, they may not like it too much.
Teacher: Oh? Maybe they don't like it.
Marcy: They don't like it, but I have to tell them because I'm older.
Teacher: The oldest person gets to be the boss?
Marcy: Yeh. That's the right way.
Teacher: So I have to watch out for the oldies, I guess, to tell me what to do.
Marcy: (Grins)

This is obviously a recurrent theme with Marcy and the teacher is giving her a lot of "space" to examine and reflect on her behavior in the group. Needless to say, this will be discussed again in later conferences.

Such self-evaluative conferences help children to grow more comfortable with their skill needs, as they and the teacher perceive them. They don't have to be defensive about poor performances. They learn to see weaknesses not as errors deserving of reproach, but rather as indicators that more work is needed. Under such conditions, the healthiest growth toward personal self-awareness and self-acceptance is fostered.

WRITTEN SELF-EVALUATION REPORTS IN THE PRIMARY GRADES

While it may seem a reach to consider using written self-evaluation reports in the primary years, they may begin as soon as children can express their thinking in writing. This will, of course, vary from class to class and from child to child, and the teacher is the best judge of when this may begin.

Written self-evaluation forms should be simple and clearly stated. They should require children to examine their work in relation to some articulated standard. These standards should not be so general as to muddy their meanings but made clear in easily understood behavioral terms. And lest they become a despised chore, they should not be required too frequently.

Self-evaluation reports may ask for information about larger learning goals. For example:

1. Tell about how you see yourself learning to:
    a. Make good observations.
    b. Carry out good investigations.
    c. Suggest good hypotheses.
    d. Work well with others in the group.
    e. Come up with good ideas.
    f. Take responsibility.
    g. Make good decisions.
2. Tell about what you think you can do best.
3. Tell about where you think you need more help.
4. Tell about your plans for next month.

(Note that the teacher phrases her requests in declarative terms, for example, "tell me about," rather than as questions, for example, "Did you take responsibility?" It is immediately clear that the declarative is softer and less confrontational than the question, making it safer for the child to respond.)

Self-evaluation reports may also address specific learning goals within a subject area.

An example for language arts:

1. Tell about:
    a. How you see yourself as a reader.
    b. How you see yourself as a story writer.
    c. How you see yourself being able to make your ideas understood.
2. Tell about your printing.
3. Tell about how you are able to record your observations.
4. Tell about what you think you can do best.
5. Tell about where you think you need more help.
6. Tell about your plans for next month in language arts.

An example for science:

1. Tell about how you see yourself as an observer in the science world.
2. Tell about your skill in
    a. Asking good questions.
    b. Gathering data.

c. Classifying data.
   d. Designing science investigations.
   e. Inventing new ways to do things.
3. Tell about what you think you can do best in science.
4. Tell about where you think you need help.
5. Tell about your plans for next month in science.

In one grade 2 class, Candice completed her self-evaluation report, commenting on how she saw her work in language arts activities:

Reading: I think I am good at reading but I could improve by [sic] *expression more. I can read smoothly.*
Listening: Most of the time I am a good listener. When I listen I know what to do.
Printing: The last 2 weeks my printing is much better them [sic] *before. I get it done too!*
Story writing: I can do good ending stories sometimes if I try.
Reports: When I do reports they are pretty good. I know how to do notes. (MacDonald, 1982)

There are many possible forms for self-evaluation reports, and what a teacher chooses to include will reflect those dimensions of learning that the teacher considers important. For as sure as the sun rises in the east, the evaluative items included will teach explicitly and implicitly what's worth knowing. There is no one perfect form, and experience in using them over time will likely result in improved practices. Input from children, both in terms of what they write and what they speak about when invited to comment, will doubtless inform future designs.

In a classroom where self-evaluation is part of the primary program experience, there are wonderful benefits in store for teachers who would choose to follow this path. Perhaps that is what makes teaching young children so satisfying. Before they become socialized to keep their opinions to themselves, they will speak the truth.

STUDENTS EVALUATING THEMSELVES IN A ONE-ON-ONE TUTORIAL

Simon was having difficulty with staying on task in his school work and his mother engaged a tutor for him so that he might be helped to focus more and pay better attention to his work. One of his more urgent needs was his lack of confidence in his ability to succeed. One-hour sessions, scheduled for twice a week, took place during the spring semester of his grade 8 year. To identify some important dimensions of his study skill work, to give him more control, and to promote his growing confidence, the tutor designed the following Self-Rating sheet for him to fill out at two-week intervals.

The issues were discussed during a self-assessment conference.

Self-Rating

1. What do you perceive to be the areas of your strengths during this last two-week period?
    a. Help me to understand by giving me some examples.
2. What do you perceive to be the areas in which you might need some help?
    a. Help me to understand by giving me some examples.
3. Here are some study skills that you use. How would you rank them in yourself, from "very strong" to "could use some work?"

5	4	3	2	1
very strong	strong	adequate	could use work	needs work
1. Belief that you can do it	5	4	3	2	1
2. Preparing:					
a. Study space	5	4	3	2	1
b. Focus	5	4	3	2	1
3. Organizing					
a. Having a plan	5	4	3	2	1
b. Not giving up when plan doesn't work	5	4	3	2	1
c. Ability to revise plan/ adapting to change	5	4	3	2	1
4. Spending time on what's important	5	4	3	2	1
5. Disciplining yourself					
a. Being clear about goals	5	4	3	2	1
b. Having an organized plan of action	5	4	3	2	1
6. Persistence/perseverance	5	4	3	2	1
7. Can analyze task into smaller, attainable elements	5	4	3	2	1
8. Able to filter out unnecessary material	5	4	3	2	1
9. Not defeated by mistakes	5	4	3	2	1
10. Can take action	5	4	3	2	1

STUDENTS EVALUATING THEMSELVES IN THE SECONDARY SCHOOL

The principles of education for secondary schools outlined by the Ministry of Education in British Columbia made clear that the issue of students' involvement in the evaluative process was an important part of their learning experiences. Teachers were encouraged to read that "as students learn how to evaluate rather than how to be evaluated, they become more skilled at reflective self-evaluation, enhancing the concept of lifelong learning. When we involve students in evaluating their own development, they have the opportunity to develop clearer concepts of themselves as learners" (B. C. Ministry of Education, 1990).

With the blessing and support of the ministry, a group of secondary school social studies teachers who initiated the use of case method teaching in their grade 11 classes, Chambers, Fukui, and Gluska (1991), created innovative assessment resources that suggested many ways in which students could be involved in self-evaluation beyond the mere issuing of grades. These teachers were committed to the belief that student involvement in their own self-assessment was an integral part of their learning goals.

Their work, represented in the document Evaluation Materials for the Graduation Program (Adam, Chambers, Fukui, Gluska & Wassermann, 1991), was made available for secondary teachers throughout the province. It will be immediately clear that these tools are useful not only for social studies but for most secondary subject areas.

Some of these resources for student self-assessments are offered below with the permission of the authors.

1. Thinking Logs. A Thinking Log is a written record of student reflection. Student reflections in a Thinking Log provide concrete evidence of how thinking processes develop over time, and how students use their thinking to examine issues of substance in class discussions. Student reflection is an ongoing process; and the recording of these reflections helps to clarify students' thinking about their work.

a. Students may take notes at the end of an assignment or project to reflect upon their research, their writing, their decision-making.
b. Students may use the margins of their notebooks to reflect on information collected during a particular class or over the course of a unit of study to engage in ongoing examination of their responses to the tasks.
c. Students may keep a separate book or section of a notebook for personal reflections. These personal reflections may be open and self-directed, or students may be given guidelines to examine specific issues.

SELF-ASSESSMENT TASK

Take the last ten minutes of class and reflect on the work you have done today. Make an entry in your Thinking Log. Be sure to date your entry. Focus your observations around one of the following:

a. What do you consider to be the most valuable issue examined today? Write about the significance of this issue in relationship to issues outside the classroom.
b. In what ways were your ideas similar to/different from those presented by other students? What points in the discussion caused you to reexamine your thinking? How comfortable were you with this process?
c. How were you able to make meaning for yourself from the information generated during today's work? Were there times when there seemed to be more information than you could digest? What strategies might you employ tomorrow to circumvent these points of "overload?"
d. If you could share some aspect of your learning today with students in another class what would you share? How would you choose to present this learning?
e. Other comments

Another type of self-assessment task is focused on a particular unit of study.

STUDENT SELF-ASSESSMENT

Topic: The Great Depression

1. Examine all the material you have on the Great Depression including notes, articles, and work samples.
2. Make an entry in your Thinking Log guided by the following questions:
    a. Describe what you have learned about the Depression. List the information from most important to least important. Relate this information to what you see as the central issues surrounding the Great Depression.
    b. What were the sources of your information? What supporting data would you consider to be based on fact? What data would you consider to be based on opinion? How comfortable are you about the accuracy of your ideas? Are there information sources that might strengthen the accuracy of your argument or point of view?

c. How did your thinking about the Great Depression change in the process of examining the issues? What factors contributed to that change? Describe the process of change as you experienced it, to the best of your ability.
d. What are your views on issues of poverty as they exist today? What evidence is there in the material from this unit that supports your view? What consequences might your beliefs have on your actions in the future?
e. What questions do you still have about the Great Depression? How might you go about finding answers to your questions?

2. Student Portfolios

Student portfolios are collections of students' work. Portfolios can contain everything the students create over the course of the semester or they can contain representative samples of what the students believe to be their best work. Students who are making the choices about what to include in their portfolios should be presented with some selection criteria to help guide their choices.

Portfolio collections encourage students to be actively involved in assessing their growth as they reflect on the materials in the portfolio. They provide material for assessments of student learning in a formative process which then gives a basis for a summative evaluation of student learning at the end of the term.

An example of a Portfolio Review:

PORTFOLIO REVIEW

Name_____ Date_____

Examine your portfolio with reference to the following:

1. What do you see as an example of the best work that you have done so far this term? What criteria have you used to make that identification?
2. Examine some recent research that you have done in your portfolio. What do you see as the strengths and weaknesses of this work? What criteria have you used to make those judgments?
3. Examine your work for evidence of changing beliefs or values. Use the self-evaluations that you have collected over the semester in your portfolio to inform your examination. To what factors would you attribute those changes?

Another example of a Portfolio Review:

PORTFOLIO REVIEW

Name _____ Date _____

1. Compare the strongest and the weakest piece of work in your portfolio. What are the significant differences? How do you explain the differences?
2. Based on your comparison, how might the weaker work be strengthened?
3. Incorporate your ideas and revise the weaker work. Submit the work to the teacher including a 50–100-word analysis of the changes you made.

3. A Summative Evaluation Report

Students are given the following self-evaluation report at the end of the semester and asked to give a summative evaluation of their work.

For example:

SUMMATIVE SELF-EVALUATION REPORT

Name _____ Date _____

This self-evaluation provides you with the opportunity to reflect upon and assess your fulfillment of the requirements of the course.

I. Fulfillment of Course Requirements

Please reflect on the extent to which you have fulfilled the course requirements. You may choose to rate yourself using the scale, or you may choose to comment, or both.

Give yourself a rating of:

1- if you believe the statement is true to a very great extent
2- if you believe the statement if generally true
3- if you believe the statement is minimally true

A. Attendance and Participation

1. My attendance in class was perfect (no missed classes for whatever reason) and I was there on time.
2. I was a very active participant in the task work groups and my contributions consistently helped the thinking of others in the group.

3. I was an active participant in class discussions and used these discussions to examine my thinking.
4. I completed all required readings and made thoughtful notes on the information read.
5. I was responsible in setting my own deadlines for the completion of my work.
6. All projects and assignments were complete and submitted on time.

B. Understanding

7. I have grown to understand the issues studied in this course. I am able to determine what are the significant factors in these issues and see their significance beyond the classroom.
8. My work in group demonstrates a genuine value for the thoughts and ideas of others.
9. I appreciate the value of self-evaluation. I am able to analyze critically my strengths and weaknesses. I think self-evaluation is an important factor in my personal growth.

II. Self-Assessment and Grading

1. Using all completed work, your portfolio, teacher's feedback, and your own evaluation responses on this Self-Evaluation, indicate what you consider to be a final grade that reflects your work in this course.

III. Open Question

Add any comments you'd like to make that have not been addressed in your responses above.

In addition to the self-evaluative resources mentioned above, Chambers, Fukui, and Gluska (1991) also designed the Profiles of Student Behaviors that represented a new and innovative approach to student self-assessment. This document was also included in the resource Evaluation Materials for the Graduate Program and made available to teachers throughout the province. It makes clear what these teachers consider to be of primary importance in student learning and, in fact, highlights their teaching goals.

It has been included here with permission from the authors. Teachers who wish to use these materials with their students have permission from the authors to duplicate them.

Profiles of Student Behaviors

Student Form
Centennial School Case Study Project
Directions

In this self-evaluation exercise, you will find twenty pairs of behavioral descriptions. Each pair is represented in two views: View A and View B, showing different views of how people learn and how they think. Your job is to decide how your behavior "matches" what is written in each profile. How do you see your behavior "fit" with the description in each of the profile views? Is your behavior more like the view shown in Profile A? Is it more like the view in Profile B? You are the one to make that decision.

As you think about each of the views in these profiles, try to decide how your behavior matches that view, in general, rather than how your behavior matches on a single day.

Read each pair of behavioral descriptions. Think about how the descriptions match your behavior. Then, try to make a judgment by choosing the number that makes the best match. You are to choose only one number on each of the profile pages. Here's how the numbers are defined:

Circle number 1, if you believe your behavior matches the description in **Profile A almost all of the time**.
Circle number 2, if you believe your behavior matches the description in **Profile A most of the time**.
Circle number 3, if you believe your behavior matches the description in **Profile A some of the time**.
Circle number 4, if you see yourself falling **right in the middle between these two views**.
Circle number 5, if you believe your behavior matches the description in **Profile B some of the time**.
Circle number 6, if you believe your behavior matches the description in **Profile B most of the time**.
Circle number 7, if you believe your behavior matches the description in **Profile B almost all of the time**.

I. Intellectual Development

1. Quality of Thinking

1.1 Can see the big ideas

View A: When you read about or listen to a topic you are able to understand the important ideas. When you present arguments or points of view, you are clear about what the important issues are.

View B: When you deal with topics or issues, you get so bogged down with the details that you miss the important ideas.

How does your behavior match these views? Circle the number that makes the best match.

1 2 3 4 5 6 7

Use the space below to add any more thoughts you have about these profiles. Provide examples from your work in the course to support your view.

I'm not rating myself in this category for this reason:

1.2 Tolerance for the ideas and opinions of others

View A: You are open to what other people think. You respect their views even if they disagree with yours. You listen closely to other people's point of view and respond to their ideas in a thoughtful and respectful way.

View B: You don't like ideas that are different from yours. You believe your ideas are the "right" ones and you find it difficult to listen to others' views. You get angry when others don't see things your way.

How does your behavior match these views? Circle the number that makes the best match.

1 2 3 4 5 6 7

Use the space below to add any more thoughts you have about these profiles. Provide examples from your work in the course to support your view.

I'm not rating myself in this category for this reason:

1.3 Knowing the difference between fact and opinion and between assumptions and fact

View A: You understand the difference between facts, assumptions, and opinions. When you present information to support your arguments, you are able to present your facts knowledgeably, and your assumptions and opinions with caution. You let people know that you are stating your opinions when you do so.

View B: You don't make much effort to show the difference between your opinions and facts when you are presenting your arguments. You don't see the need to make it clear that you are presenting your own opinions. Your opinions and the assumptions you make are as good as facts to you.

How does your behavior match these views? Circle the number that makes the best match.

1 2 3 4 5 6 7

Use the space below to add any more thoughts you have about these profiles. Provide examples from your work in the course to support your view.

I'm not rating myself in this category for this reason:

1.4 Tolerance for contrary data

View A: Even though you may believe something very strongly, you are usually able to consider different points of view. When you are faced with information that is different from what you believe, you examine it thoughtfully and carefully to see how it fits in with your thinking.

View B: Once you believe something to be true, you do not find it necessary to consider any other point of view. You don't see the need to continue thinking about an issue once you have figured out what you believe to be the right answer.

How does your behavior match these views? Circle the number that makes the best match.
   1   2   3   4   5   6   7

Use the space below to add any more thoughts you have about these profiles. Provide examples from your work in the course to support your view.

I'm not rating myself in this category for this reason:

1.5 Examples that support ideas

View A: When you are asked to provide examples to support your arguments, you are able to do so without difficulty. What's more, the examples you choose are clearly related to what you are saying.

View B: You are unable to find examples to support your arguments. You believe that your arguments don't need to be defended with examples.

How does your behavior match these views? Circle the number that makes the best match.
   1   2   3   4   5   6   7

Use the space below to add any more thoughts you have about these profiles. Provide examples from your work in the course to support your view.

I'm not rating myself in this category for this reason:

1.6 Intelligent interpretation of data

View A: You are able to understand what you have heard, or observed, and you are able to communicate that understanding to others. What's more, you are cautious about drawing conclusions about what you have heard or seen when there is insufficient evidence.

View B: You jump to conclusions without having adequate data to back them up and may twist information to support your ideas.

How does your behavior match these views? Circle the number that makes the best match.

1 2 3 4 5 6 7

Use the space below to add any more thoughts you have about these profiles. Provide examples from your work in the course to support your view.

I'm not rating myself in this category for this reason:

1.7 Original, inventive, creative work

View A: You are able to go beyond what is ordinary and create new ideas and products. You are original and inventive and what comes out of you is fresh, new, and imaginative. You are able to take risks and push yourself to the limits of creativity.

View B: You feel more comfortable sticking with ways of doing things that are routine and have worked for you in the past. The idea of change makes you feel uncomfortable.

How does your behavior match these views? Circle the number that makes the best match.

1 2 3 4 5 6 7

Use the space below to add any more thoughts you have about these profiles. Provide examples from your work in the course to support your view.

I'm not rating myself in this category for this reason:

1.8 Embracing thinking as a way of life

View A: You value thinking as a way of solving problems and as a way of making decisions. You want to think for yourself and you want to think your own ideas. You are independent and view thinking as a tool to enrich your life.

View B: You would rather have someone tell you what to do and believe than have to do the thinking for yourself. You believe it is the teacher's job to do the thinking and the student's job to follow orders.

How does your behavior match these views? Circle the number that makes the best match.

1 2 3 4 5 6 7

Use the space below to add any more thoughts you have about thee profiles. Provide examples from your work in the course to support your view.

I'm not rating myself in this category for this reason:

II. Skills

2. Communication of Ideas

2.1 Quality of thinking in writing

View A: Your written ideas are presented clearly and are based on many different sources of information including facts, observations, details, and statistics. You are able to provide examples that clarify what you mean. Your writing is well organized. You use well-constructed sentences and give thought to spelling, punctuation, and capitalization. You are able to communicate ideas in a way that is interesting to the reader.

View B: You are unable to express your thoughts in writing. This happens either because you are unable to organize your ideas in your head or because when you do get them organized, you are unable to transfer the information to the written page.

How does your behavior match these views? Circle the number that makes the best match.
  1 2 3 4 5 6 7

Use the space below to add any more thoughts you have about these profiles. Provide examples from your work in the course to support your view.

I'm not rating myself in this category for this reason:

2.2 Quality of thinking in speaking

View A: When you make an oral presentation, your language is clear, and you support your ideas with data. Your ideas are interesting, and it is easy for others to understand what you are saying. When you argue your point of view, you make sense.

View B: You have difficulty with oral presentations. You are unable to articulate your ideas so they make sense to the listener. They come out as unconnected thoughts and are often not adequately supported with data.

How does your behavior match these views? Circle the number that makes the best match.
  1 2 3 4 5 6 7

Use the space below to add any more thoughts you have about these profiles. Provide examples from your work in the course to support your view.

I'm not rating myself in this category for this reason:

3. Research Skills

3.1 Collecting and organizing information

View A: You are able to locate and gather data from many sources. When you use the information you have collected in your oral or written work, it is organized in a way that makes sense and focuses on the important issues. You use the information you collect to examine all sides of an issue and draw your conclusions based on this balanced examination. You are clear about what constitutes information and what are distortions of the truth. You use a fact check to ensure that your information is verifiable.

View B: When you prepare for a report or speech, you rely heavily on one source of information. Often when you search for background material at the library, you come up empty-handed. Your reports usually take one side of an issue and sometimes you miss the important points altogether. You use information that is not verifiable, and you fail to use fact-checking to ensure your information is solid.

How does your behavior match these views? Circle the number that makes the best match.

1 2 3 4 5 6 7

Use the space below to add any more thoughts you have about these profiles. Provide examples from your work in the course to support your view.

I'm not rating myself in this category for this reason:

3.2 Extracting and recording information

View A: When you research a topic, you use a variety of sources and you are able to gather the information that zeroes in on the important issues. You are cautious about using sources from the Internet, and use "fact-checking" to ensure that what you extract is bona fide and not disinformation. You don't have difficulty differentiating between what is important and what may be left out. You are able to record the information you gathered in a way that makes sense. You are careful about citing the sources you used and don't pass off other people's work as your own.

View B: When you do research for a project, you collect large volumes of information. You are unable to separate what's important from what is unimportant. You rely on single sources, like the Internet, and you are not careful about fact-checking for truth and disinformation. You end up working with large amounts of material, some of which is unverified, and your report lacks focus.

How does your behavior match these views? Circle the number that makes the best match.

1 2 3 4 5 6 7

Use the space below to add any more thoughts you have about these profiles. Provide examples from your work to support your view.

I'm not rating myself in this category for this reason:

4. Interpersonal Skills

4.1 Attends to the ideas of others

View A: In a group discussion, you are able to listen carefully to the ideas of other students and hear what they are saying. The way you respond to them lets them know that you have heard them and understood what they have said.

View B: When someone is speaking, you are so busy trying to figure out what you are going to say that you are unable to listen to the speaker. Your reply does not relate to what the speaker said. When you get your turn, you just want to present your own ideas. It is more important for you to get your own ideas out than to hear the ideas of others.

How does your behavior match these views? Circle the number that makes the best match.

1 2 3 4 5 6 7

Use the space below to add any more thoughts you have about these profiles. Provide examples from your work in class to support your view.

I'm not rating myself in this category for this reason:

4.2 Contributes to the facilitation of group discussion

View A: When working in a group, you listen carefully to the ideas of other students even if the ideas expressed do not agree with your own. It's easy for you to be respectful of the ideas of others and to show that respect in your group discussions. You take an active part in making sure that the group discussion is productive, and that is more important to you than getting out your own ideas.

View B: Working in a group is difficult for you. You become frustrated with ideas that are different from yours. It is very important that you get your own ideas out. You usually take up most of the talk time in the group and you don't really care about squeezing out other members.

How does your behavior match these views? Circle the number that makes the best match.

1 2 3 4 5 6 7

Use the space below to add any more thoughts you have about these profiles. Provide examples from your work in the course to support our view.

I'm not rating myself in this category for this reason:

III. Attitudes

5. Personal Perspectives

5.1 Positive world outlook

View A: You see problems as challenges. When faced with a problem, you feel good about your ability to solve it. You like to challenge yourself, and even when you are not successful in solving a problem, you are able to keep your confidence as a problem-solver.

View B: When you are faced with a new problem, you just assume that you can't do it. Instead of putting your energy into solving a problem, you are more likely to complain about your situation. You don't see how problems can be solved, and taking action on a problem is not what you would choose to do.

How does your behavior match these views? Circle the number that makes the best match.

1 2 3 4 5 6 7

Use the space below to add any more thoughts you have about these profiles. Provide examples from your work in the course to support your view.

I'm not rating myself in this category for this reason:

5.2 Tolerance for ambiguity

View A: When you are faced with conflicting information, you are patient and you are able to wait to make a decision until better information is available. When you face a situation that appears to be neither right nor wrong, that does not make you uncomfortable. You are comfortable even when the "answers" have not been found.

View B: You are very uncomfortable with situations that have no "right" or "wrong" answers. You need to see answers found. You see things as either true or false; good or bad; right or wrong. This helps you to know what is what! You have a great deal of difficulty in leaving things open, and it really drives you crazy when the issues are not resolved.

How does your behavior match these views? Circle the number that makes the best match.

1 2 3 4 5 6 7

Use the space below to add any more thoughts you have about these profiles. Provide examples from your work in the course to support your view.

I'm not rating myself in this category for this reason:

5.3 World perspective

View A: When you examine an issue, you are able to see how it affects other people in your school, community, or city. You realize how your school and your community are related to the whole world, and you appreciate all people as part of a world community.

View B: You see events in terms of how they affect you personally. World events like famine, war, homelessness are someone else's problems.

How does your behavior match these views? Circle the number that makes the best match.

1 2 3 4 5 6 7

Use the space below to add any more thoughts you have about these profiles. Provide examples from your work in the course to support your view.

I'm not rating myself in this category for this reason:

6. Beliefs and Values

6.1 Your beliefs inform your behavior

View A: You think about what you believe and you really are clear about what is important to you. There is a clear connection between what you believe and how you act. Your actions over time are a clear reflection of your values.

View B: You are unclear about what you believe, and if asked about what is important to you, you don't really know, because you haven't thought this out. How you act does not seem connected to what you believe.

How does your behavior match these views? Circle the number that makes the best match.

1 2 3 4 5 6 7

Use the space below to add any more thoughts you have about these profiles. Provide examples from your work in the course to support your view.

I'm not rating myself in this category for this reason:

7. Self-Evaluation

7.1 Open to self-evaluation

View A: You welcome the chance to evaluate your own work. You see self-evaluation as a chance to learn more about yourself, as an opportunity to examine your strengths and weaknesses, and determine where more work is needed. You are not afraid to be honest in owning up to where you are having trouble. This ability to look at yourself honestly allows you to be more open to learning.

View B: Evaluation is the teacher's job. You think that's what teachers get paid for. You find it uncomfortable and difficult to examine something you have done. You learn more when someone else does the evaluation for you.

How does your behavior match these views? Circle the number that makes the best match.

1   2   3   4   5   6   7

Use the space below to add any more thoughts you have about these profiles. Provide examples from your work in the course to support your view.

I'm not rating myself in this category for this reason:

7.2 Skill in self-evaluation

View A: You are able to look at your own work critically. You are thoughtful when you examine your work, and you can see your strengths and weaknesses realistically. You can recognize where you need help, and you are able to ask for that help as part of the process of learning.

View B: You are unable to look at your work critically. Looking at yourself critically leaves you open to criticism that you like to avoid. Instead of owning up to your own learning needs, you are likely to blame others, or distort the facts, rather than acknowledge your shortcomings.

How does your behavior match these views? Circle the number that makes the best match.

1   2   3   4   5   6   7

Use the space below to add any more thoughts you have about these profiles. Provide examples from your work in the course to support your view.

I'm not rating myself in this category for this reason:

TEACHERS' ASSESSMENTS ON THE PROFILES

The additive feature in the use of the profiles was a teacher's version that was completed by the teacher for all students. In a one-on-one conference, discrepancies between the two forms were examined, and students asked to comment about them, in the presence of teacher responses that called for reexamination, and perhaps a citing of examples that supported or questioned the student's view. In the conference, the teacher was careful to use facilitative responses and questions rather than "shaming and blaming" so that students might reengage in a more honest and accurate self-assessment.

CONCLUSION

This chapter has offered a breakfast buffet of the kinds of evaluation tools that teachers have used, in primary, intermediate, and secondary classes, to engage students in self-assessment. In all cases, it has been the teacher, or groups of teachers, who have designed the self-rating forms. They begin with the identification of what the teacher sees as the important dimensions of the performance as they relate to grade or subject standards. In each case, it is clear that the self-assessments contain references not only to understandings and skills but also to more personal aspects of the way students see themselves in relation to their studies.

For teachers who are considering such a course of action, it is hoped that the above examples will illuminate the how and the what of designing self-assessment forms.

Not every first attempt may be successful—but the feedback from students and the teacher's own self-assessment of the success of the forms should lead to further editing, resulting in sufficient improvements as to render them more than profitable.

Rick Stiggins (2009) in his helpful article, "Assessment FOR Learning in Upper Elementary Grades," reminds teachers, in using assessment:

"How can we ensure that the emotional dynamics of the assessment experience for upper elementary students leaves them willing to risk trying?

How can we keep them from giving up on themselves so early in their academic lives?"

One answer is surely to incorporate self-assessment as a normal part of classroom work at every level of educational experience.

Teachers who have used these tools in the past point to their value, not only in promoting more fair and accurate judgments about students' work but, even more important, in making a substantial contribution to students' self-awareness and subsequent empowerment.

Chapter 10

Institutional Changes toward Using Evaluative Feedback in Reporting to Parents

One of the most formidable challenges to changes in student assessment has to lie at the doorstep of parents, especially those who are obsessively concerned with how their children "rank" and how these rankings will affect their future admission into select colleges and universities. Such a challenge cannot be ignored, for if any change is to be successful, it has to begin with acknowledgment of the impediments and the ways in which they can be addressed.

It should come as no surprise that parents who are overly obsessed with their children's grades have gone to great lengths to insure their offspring's preferred place in institutions of higher learning. This is not a matter of education; it is a sign of unhealth, a desperate means to get to the top of the ladder.

More recently, it has been disclosed that to secure privileged placements for their children at select colleges and universities, nineteen parents pleaded guilty in a college admissions bribery fraud that involved rigging test scores and bribing coaches in order to gain entry to Yale and Georgetown. According to the *New York Times*, at least twenty people were involved in a college admissions bribery scandal that attempted to influence undergraduate decisions at several top American universities (Taylor and Bosman, 2019).

Introducing a change in the "mighty fortress" of a school system without prior consultation with and education of the parent group may be doomed from the start.

Given all of that, change must begin with educating parents to the *raison d'etre* of the need for change, why the change is an improvement and what the limitations and impediments of the old system are. Parent education may not be overlooked or ignored in what, to them, is likely to be a sea change in practice. This is probably true for any radical change proposed by the school or district. Getting the parents on side will ease the process considerably (see, for example, Bernard and Boothby, 2019).

Not all parents are addicted to the numbers and letters game. Many informed parents have already understood and are appreciative participants in a system that evaluates students with teachers' commentaries that address those students' strengths and areas of needed help, as reflected by the standards of the grade or the subject. This kind of assessment gives parents a more focused and more comprehensible look at what they might do, as partners in their children's learning, to help and support them.

Many private schools in the United States have been using evaluative assessments for many years—and some individual public schools have "gone their own way" in using evaluative comments rather than grades. It might come as a shock to learn that parents actively seek out these public schools, since they already understand the merits of evaluative assessment over ranking. More importantly, several large school districts are now moving toward evaluative feedback in lieu of grades; the motivating factors seem to lie in the realm of what is now available for our youth in the IT world. More about this in the sections below.

EXAMPLES OF SCHOOLS THAT "DARE TO BE DIFFERENT"

a. The Dwight-Englewood School

The Dwight-Englewood School is a private K-12 school in Englewood, New Jersey. It has long ago eschewed letter and number grades on report cards to parents in favor of emphasis on comments, in addition to providing a grid with check marks that assess whether the student is working "satisfactorily, progressing, or needs more effort" in selected subject areas that include science, art, language arts, and general learning and social skills.

In each grid, the standards are listed. For example, the language arts grid includes standards of reading fluency, expression and comprehension, creative writing, essay writing, vocabulary, and spelling. In the category of "general learning and social skills," the standards include listening, following directions, commitment to task, organization of time and materials, completion of assignments, ability to work independently, cooperation, neatness of work, courtesy and consideration for others, and effort. Check marks indicate whether the student is doing adequate work or needs improvement.

The comments provide further elaboration of what is contained in the grid.

Parents who pay tuition for their children to attend Dwight-Englewood fully accept the reporting system. There is no outcry or protest over the lack of numbers of symbols that rank the students. The reporting system is part of the "package" that parents subscribe to when enrolling their children.

b. Charles Dickens Elementary School and Annex

The Charles Dickens Elementary School is a public school in east Vancouver. Although it is now in a new, more modern building, it had, for more than eighty years, been a red-brick relic from the early days of public education in the city. The school enrolls a diverse mix of ethnic groups, typical of the lower-middle-class neighborhood. Many children are new Canadians; some speak English as yet haltingly, others not quite yet. Children in a single class come from El Salvador, Honduras, India, Canada, Portugal, China, Vietnam, the Philippines, and Ireland. Some of the children identified as Canadians are of First Nations heritage.

Charles Dickens is not the school one would have picked to defy every new curriculum *du jour* handed down by school boards and the Ministry of Education over the last forty years. It is not the school that one would have picked to remain true to its child-centered roots, facing off against such educational tsunamis as the back-to-basics movement, Madeline Hunter's direct instruction, and, more recently, the high stakes testing madness that passes for educational quality. And this is certainly not the school, given the challenges of the student population, that one would have picked to demonstrate such high-performance levels in the student population, showing once again what many educators have long known: that given the "right stuff"—the right teachers, the right administration, the right conditions—all children can be successful learners (Wassermann, 2007).

In addition to enrolling students from the neighborhood, the school is also a magnet for parents throughout the city who prefer their children to be in a school where the teaching and the programs are child-centered and that does not change their philosophy from decade to decade. In fact, there is a waiting list for students who come from outside the school catchment area.

The tradition here is solid; the school knows what it stands for, and it is unwavering in its orientation to the education, health and welfare of its students. When parents enroll their children at Charles Dickens, they are handed a brochure with the mission statement of the school, developed by previous principals, staff, and a group of parents. The brochure includes a list of beliefs that underlie the operating practices of the school:

- Learning requires the active participation of the learner.
- People learn in different ways and at different rates.
- Learning is built on individual and social processes.
- The learner is the focus of education, not the curriculum.

- The integration of subjects is necessary.
- Creativity and critical problem-solving skills should be taught.
- Curiosity, creativity, and cooperation should be nurtured.
- Play is a condition of learning.
- Questions should be valued.
- A sense of responsibility in decision making should be fostered.
- A sense of self as an individual and as part of the group is important.

Some have asked how it is possible, in large school district, where there is city, school board, and provincial government control over standards, curriculum mandates, and, in some cases, teaching strategies, that a school like Dickens is able to retain its commitment to its own beliefs.

The child-centered program at Dickens was initiated in 1988, when the then principal, George Rooney, requested that the school be granted status as an "alternative school." This designation gave them more degrees of freedom and allowed them to depart, in giant steps, from mainstream practices seen throughout the district. Standardized tests used in Vancouver and in other provincial district schools were rejected in favor of the professional judgments of teachers. Now that alternative school status is no longer necessary. The school has proved itself many times over and has become a lighthouse school for child-centered education.

When the new principal, John Perpich, was asked as to how it was possible for Dickens to retain its singular position in the district, he said, "Of course we are required to document a student's level of achievement. And as long as I can document a child's progress and successful performance, 'downtown' is happy. Of course, there are many ways to do this" (Wassermann, 2009). Dickens continues to march to the drummers of its own educational beliefs.

The teachers in Dickens primary school remain with the same group of children for three years. In this way, they get to know the students better and become more familiar with their individual learning needs and styles. There is no grade-level curriculum that is enforced; each child's learning needs are met along a continuum of progress. In this system, no child is a failure who would be subject to ridicule. Perpich noted that the school does not use a deficit model of evaluation; instead, the emphasis is on efficacy and success.

There are no grades given at Dickens. Parents receive anecdotal reports written by the teachers. Attached to these reports are students' self-evaluations of their work. Both the principal and the teachers have observed that in such a climate of openness and respect, children evaluate themselves with great honesty and perception.

The parents' responses to narrative reporting indicate their preference to it. They claim that the narratives tell them much more than letter grades. A very few parents do still ask for letter grades, however, and the school does provide them if requested, thus obviating any protests. However, such requests are rare.

Over the years, interviews with teachers, principals, parents, and district officials has provided a richly textured view of how a school with a highly challenging population has not only survived but flourished. What happens when Dickens' students enter the more rigid secondary schools in the city? The feedback from secondary teachers accepting Dickens' students is that these young people are well rounded, can carry on good discussions focused on the "big ideas," are good leaders, are good team players, are autonomous, flexible, make good adjustments to high school, and are personally responsible (Wassermann, 2007). Such reports remind one of the descriptions of the high school graduates from the Eight-Year Study program, carried out in 1932–1940 (Aikens, 1948).

Children who enroll in Charles Dickens Elementary School begin with their attendance at the Annex, for grades K-3. At this point, parents are given a booklet that contains an overview of their singular assessment and reporting scheme (Vancouver School Board, 2018). This booklet outlines the standards against which primary students are evaluated, as well as the means of evaluation. While this booklet can be downloaded, for convenience it is extracted here:

Teaching and Learning Assessment and Reporting

Charles Dickens Elementary School Annex (December 6, 2018)

Communicating Student Learning on a regular and ongoing basis allows both learners and parents to gauge where the student is in the learning, what they are working toward, and the ways in which learning is supported. By their own participation in the process, students are provided with meaningful information or feedback about their learning so that they can monitor their progress toward the learning goals they have set. Parents are involved as partners in a dialogue about their child's progress and the best ways to support and improve learning.

The communication of student learning to parents is based on clear standards and expectations and is intended to make learning visible. This continuous window into their child's progress encourages them to take an active part by working closely with teachers to help ensure their child's success. Students are encouraged to think of questions: Where am I now? Where am I going? What do I need to do to get there?

There will be a new reporting schedule

The new reporting practice will include five required communications with parents within a calendar year:

- A minimum of **three** ongoing communications with families (timing at the teacher's discretion)
- **Two** formal written reports:
   A Progress Report that will be sent home to families **by the end of January**.
- This report will indicate where the child is in relation to the age/grade expectations using written comments and a competency scale.
- A summary of the progress toward the goals in the child's Individual Education Plan (IEP), that will be sent home to families by the end of June.
   A Summative Report that will be sent home to families **by the end of June**.
- This report will indicate where the child is in relation to the age/grade expectations using written comments and a competency scale and student self-assessment of the Core Competencies (Communication, Thinking, and Personal and Social)
- Letter grades are provided to parents on request.
   If you have any questions, feel free to contact your child's teacher or the school office.
   (https://www.vsb.bc.ca/schools/charles-dickens-annex/Teaching and Learning Pages/defalut.aspx)

c. Little Red Schoolhouse

The Little Red Schoolhouse (and its secondary partner, Elizabeth Irwin) is located on Bleecker Street, in Greenwich Village, New York City. It opened its doors in 1921, founded by Elizabeth Irwin, and is regarded as the city's first progressive education establishment, based on the principles and practices of John Dewey. There are no grades (e.g., grades 1, 2, 3, 4, 5, 6) in LR; children are grouped by age. The secondary school, Elizabeth Irwin, begins with grade 7 through grade 12. LREI does not shrink from identifying itself as a pre-K-12 progressive education institution.

There is a long waiting list for parents who wish to enroll their children in LREI, and the school's history would indicate that parents who choose LREI are more likely to be considered as "progressives" in their political and social orientation. It would not come as a surprise, then, to know that from its beginnings LREI has rejected the use of formal report cards, and, instead, uses narratives to report to parents about their children's work and progress. At both Little Red and Elizabeth Irwin, the student is an important participant in the assessment process.

As a matter of interest, recent (2017) graduates from LREI have gone on to placements at New York University, Boston University, California Institute of the Arts, Duke, Princeton, Bennington, Bard, Skidmore, Ithaca, Northwestern, Sarah Lawrence, Brown, Cornell, Wesleyan, and Vassar—to name a few. Such indicators give the lie to the necessity of letter and number grades as imperative for college and university acceptance.

One needn't go to the elite private schools and alternate schools to find the shift from letter and number grades to narrative reports.

d. New York City and beyond

Kyle Spencer, reporting in the *New York Times* (2017), writes about the new program in the New York City public schools that is challenging the way teachers and students think about academic accomplishments. For example, in Brooklyn, Middle School 442 encourages students to focus on mastering sets of grade-level skills, moving ahead to the next set of skills when they have demonstrated they are ready. In these schools, "there is no such thing as a C or a D for a lazily written term paper. There is no failing. The only goal is to learn the material sooner or later" (Spencer, 2017).

Spencer adds that "mastery learning, also known as competency-based learning, is taking hold across the country" and writes that more than forty schools in New York City have adopted the program—a grassroots movement in which schools voluntarily shift gears from letter and number grades to mastery learning. This shift has been attributed to several factors, including the rise of online learning, new technologies, new education software, and computer-assisted teaching.

Despite being labor intensive for teachers, mastery learning offers students more agency and allows them to "gain traction, no matter their level." The approach puts the focus on student growth and suggests that it is most beneficial for at-risk students and those who have become disenchanted with school. "In New York City, where students speak more than 200 different languages and arrive in classrooms with varying degrees of proficiency, some schools have adopted the method out of necessity" (Spencer, 2017).

Despite its critics, at Brooklyn's Middle School 442 all the eighth graders who took the algebra Regents exam and 85 percent who took the earth science exam were marked proficient. Reading scores improved significantly, as did proficiency in English. According to the Hechinger Report (https://hechingerreport.org/special-reports/), "the factory model of education is out.

Now more schools are personalizing learning and trying to motivate them by empowering them in the classroom." Perhaps this can be classified under the rubric, "Will wonders never cease?"

Vermont, Maine, and New Hampshire have now passed laws requiring school districts to phase in mastery learning. Ten school districts in Illinois, including Chicago, are introducing this approach. In 2014, the Idaho state legislature approved nineteen programs to explore the practice (Spencer, 2017) (see also, Cuban, "Reforming Student Report Cards," July 11, 2019, https://larrycuban.wordpress.com/).

As Lindsey Own (2015) from Shoreline, Washington, has written, "Teachers at my school don't give grades. Instead we write narratives describing to parents and other stakeholders how our students are progressing on learning objectives. These are time-consuming to write and can sometimes be not exceptionally clear to parents—we need to work on using less teacher-language and be more specific in explaining progress with fewer superlatives. But I strongly believe that this kind of reporting is much more effective than percentages and letters and I've been thrilled to hear from more and more colleagues in public and independent schools that the broader mindset in education is shifting in the direction of narrative rather than number grades."

There is a danger to this kind of holus-bolus attempt to make a sea change in a deeply entrenched system, and there is much evidence in the history of educational reform that shows how best efforts to make improvements have failed for numbers of reasons. Education has had a sordid history of taking two giant steps forward and five back in educational reform (see, e.g., Cuban and Tyack, 1997; Cuban, 2013).

There are several reasons to explain this—not the least being teachers' lack of understanding of how the "theories" behind the change may be applied in classroom practice, combined with poor-quality professional development for teachers to help them understand the "how" as well as the "why." In order for the change to endure, teachers must not only subscribe to it in terms of their beliefs, but also must understand the "how" of the practices as well as see evidence of its success. Otherwise, these too, like other innovative programs of the past, may be doomed to fail.

e. British Columbia, Canada

It may be a truism to suggest that the changes being seen in school programs and in the manner of assessment are intimately connected to the profound influence of the high-tech world in which we live. And it may also be a truism that students today are more connected to that world than many of the adults in their immediate circle. What has been noted is that technology is making it possible for teachers to differentiate and tailor instruction to individual student needs, motivating them and creating resources that personalize learning.

School districts in more than a few areas are now struggling to devise new programs and new assessment strategies that are more in accord with what students can accomplish outside of school. In other words, if schools are to retain their agency in educating young people, if they are not going to be replaced by tablets with programs designed to do, at home, what teachers could do at school, then perhaps it is time for school districts to pull up their socks and, as the kids would say, "get in the ball game." If high tech is the strong motivator for more personalized teaching and learning, then kudos to them.

The Ministry of Education in British Columbia has now issued a new directive that will be responsible for informing new and innovative practices in schoolrooms across the province. According to their website, "The education system is being modernized and as part of this process, new curriculum is being introduced in all B.C. schools" (https://www2.gov.bc.ca/). The new program is based on the ministry's data gathering with educators and puts emphasis on student involvement in the learning process, with attention to higher-order critical and creative thinking skills.

As part of this new initiative, the ministry surveyed teachers and parents throughout the province about assessment and used that data to inform the new assessment guidelines. There were several reasons that participants in the survey supported the continued use of letter grades and percentages and several reasons that participants opposed the continued use of letter grades. However, both groups wanted to see additional context provided through personalized comments from teachers. Some respondents noted that letter grades and percentages should not be used in earlier grades.

All respondents emphasized the need for more personalization and more frequency in teachers' comments. In particular, they requested that report card comments contain more plain language and less jargon and "cookie cutter" wording, noting that generic comments do not provide enough concrete feedback to help a student or guide a parent in helping his or her child to improve. Parents also said that they wanted teachers to be candid in their feedback, rather than glossing over a child's weaknesses (British Columbia Ministry of Education, https:www2.gov.bc.ca).

Although parents did acknowledge the amount of time it takes teachers to write such reports, they nevertheless said they wanted to feel like the teacher knows and understands the needs, strengths, and weakness of each child. In helping teachers make these assessments, the ministry provided a clear and unambiguous list of competencies in each subject area for each grade.

Based upon the new program from the ministry, the Vancouver School Board initiated a pilot program to test "a new way of assessing students"

(Bernard and Boothby, 2019). Letter and number grades have been eliminated in elementary grades in favor of written assessments, or "narratives" that are based upon goals and standards for each grade that emphasize communication, thinking, and social competencies. Zerbe, a director of instruction at the Vancouver School Board, says that the new way of assessment outlines what areas the student needs to develop and what the student could do to become proficient (Bernard and Boothby, 2019).

So far, the feedback from parents and teachers has been positive. "Teachers report they like the personalized approach and are now able to comment on things that matter in the child's learning. Parents have reported that they like the improved communication with teachers" (Bernard and Boothby, 2019). Zerbe anticipates that the new report card will be officially adopted by the rest of the province in the next few years.

f. Simon Fraser University, Faculty of Education: Teacher Education Program

When the teacher education program was created in 1965, at the opening of a new provincial university, built on the top of Burnaby Mountain, in the eastern part of the city of Vancouver, the then dean, Archie MacKinnon, was committed to a radical and innovative change in the way teachers were to be prepared. Instead of a series of courses that mounted up in a collection of course credits, and led to a final practicum, MacKinnon, in a bold and radical shift, created a three-semester program that began with an eight-week practicum, followed by coursework in the second semester and ending with a full sixteen-week practicum.

It was a major shift in thinking about teacher education and in program design. It would not be an exaggeration to note that the venerable institution across town, University of British Columbia, predicted that the new program would collapse after a brief term. With a lot of smirking and sarcasm, the accredited and tenured professors in that faculty chorused that such "idiotic" ideas were doomed to fail.

In the now fifty plus years since the program was created, the Professional Development Program at Simon Fraser University has become the leading and highest-honored teacher education program in Canada with not a few Canadian universities following suit.

But more to the point. In the very beginning, students were given letter grades for both the first and the final practicum, as well as for the second semester's course work. It became clear, however, that such a system of assessment was incongruous with the innovative nature of the program. A proposal was then put forth to change the letter grade assessments to a

Pass-Withdraw system, based upon articulated standards specified in the *Profiles of Student Competencies* (Wassermann and Eggert, 1976, 1981).

The profiles described, in paragraph form, nineteen specific teacher competencies that would be necessary for successful classroom teaching. Each student would complete the student form of the profiles and the instructor would also complete the teacher form. In a conference, the two assessments would be compared, and an overall positive assessment would entitle the student to a Pass. There would be no Failing grade. The rationale for that was that a student who was "not cut out for teaching" would not be a failure, but perhaps more suited to another profession. Not everyone is suited for teaching, which does not mean that person is a failure. Withdraw seemed a more appropriate assessment for this radical new program that emphasized the importance of growth and learning as a teacher.

The proposal for this change in assessment first was presented to the members of the Faculty of Education at a regular faculty meeting. Its approval was not unanimous; but it did squeak by. For its further acceptance, it had to be presented to the Faculty Senate. After considerable discussion and several strong opposers, the proposal was passed. And the Pass-Withdraw system became the assessment protocol for the Professional Development Program.

It would be fair to say that the program has been strengthened by such an assessment system and other faculties of education in Canada, while not following suit, have no longer smirked or forecast failure, while looking in admiration at the success of the program that has produced a crop of outstanding teachers over the last fifty-five years.

CONCLUSION

Efforts to change the deeply entrenched systems of education practice have, over the last hundred years, borne little fruit. Over the years, reforms have come, and they have gone; in fact, the nature of change in educational practice seems to be remarkably like a revolving door. Curriculum reforms stemming back to the initiatives based on John Dewey's work in the 1930s advocating more child-centered practices breezed in and out so fast, it was hardly noticed.

New curriculum materials, bought with meager funds, rarely saw the light of day. iPads bought for every student in the Los Angeles school district were used by children to surf the Internet and the cost and misuse of the tablets led to the resignation of the superintendent of schools. Open school designs that were intended to foster more teacher collaboration quickly gave way to screens put up to isolate the classes into self-contained units.

Who remembers the Initial Teaching Alphabet? Madeline Hunter's "direct instruction?" The "new math?" "Individualized Reading?" The British Primary School model? The ungraded classroom? Open schools, child-centered schools, open classrooms, organic primary programs all had their heyday and vanished, like some discarded offal. Larry Cuban, who has written much about educational reform, has noted that "the apparent uniformity in instruction irrespective of time and place appears connected to the apparent invulnerability of classrooms to change" (Cuban, 2008).

Now, with a mind to what the information technology world has made available to most students in first-world countries, there appears yet a new shift—toward practices and curriculum materials that are more compatible with the twenty-first century's mandates. Student-centered learning, learning at one's own pace, learning without the threat of a bad letter grade, learning higher-order thinking skills, and better means of communication are now becoming the *plat du jour* of the new curriculum.

Along with these "new" programs come assessment initiatives that are more compatible with these new programs, that is, the rejection of letter and number grades, at least in the elementary school, in favor of "narratives" or anecdotal reporting, measured against clearly identified grade-level standards. Will it endure? If history tells us anything about school reform, the chances don't seem promising. But hey, that reform history does not reflect our new age where nearly every youngster has his or her own tablet, and access to a wide variety of learning apps that teach understandings, concepts, and skills in the absence of a teacher. As one-third grader remarked, as he was whipping through information on his tablet, "I've been doing this since I was three years old."

This signifies that there is hope that the removal of letters and numbers, deeply embedded in the history of our industrial age, will be phased out—this time, for good. At the least, the evidence is clear that those schools, private and public, that have abandoned that system in favor of narratives have not, as predicted, fallen into the abyss of unworthy, disreputable places with low-performance graduates. In fact, the data reveal that the opposite is true.

So yes, there is hope for "evaluation without tears" and for teachers and schools and school systems who are moving to embrace that change. And for those who are seeking to move in that direction, the beacons of schools who have done so in the past may serve as guiding lights to enable, encourage, and support them.

Chapter 11

Evaluation as a Subversive Activity
What Can a Teacher Do?

When Neil Postman and Charles Weingartner wrote their seminal book *Teaching as a Subversive Activity* (1969), they most likely took their ideas from their observations of what teachers did in classrooms that ran countercurrent to established practices. The book "spoke" to many teachers who were already engaged in covertly using teaching practices that were radical, innovative, different, and more student-centered than the "norm." In other words, even a generation ago, classroom teachers found ways to inject more relevant teaching practices into the dry, humdrum, mundane life of classrooms.

The teachers who did this created materials and used strategies that were more in accord with their beliefs about what education could be, should be—in other words, what was "right and good" for the health, welfare, and education of their students. The authors described what teachers did who were committed to more student-centered practices, with emphasis on the ways in which they managed to do this within the constraints of what was prescribed and proscribed. As Tyack and Cuban (1995) have pointed out, "It is precisely because the age-graded school also permits teachers to have their own classrooms to which doors are attached that give teachers a freedom to change, to alter existing practices."

This chapter is for teachers who continue to teach in those districts and schools that have, so far, not been moved to change their evaluation practices. It is especially for those teachers who see the urgent need to evaluate student learning that does not demean them, crush their spirits, or punish them for their failings. How can such teachers use more effective and child-centered evaluation practices within the parameters set up by their schools, districts, departments of education?

What is being proposed here is likely not as exotic or radical as to make a teacher vulnerable. But if we can't have it all, perhaps we can take some important steps that are more in keeping with evaluation without tears.

a. Using Regular Student Self-Evaluations as an Integral Part of Student Learning

All evaluation begins from the point of knowing and recognizing that there are standards and "benchmarks" that are assigned to a subject, a course, a grade level, or, in some cases, a performance. Those standards should be made clear to students, even to those in the primary years. When the goals and standards are clear, students know what they are aiming for in their learning and what they are going to be assessed against.

It may be important for these grade or subject-area goals to be made explicit—perhaps in the form of a printout for both students and parents. They are often specified by the district or the school, or the department of education, but a teacher should feel free to modify the language so that it is clearly understandable by students and parents. These goals and standards then become the template for the ongoing self-assessment of the students.

Of course, the teacher may wish to inject some of his or her own goals or standards into the list, perhaps those that have been overlooked by the establishment, but are, nevertheless, of importance to the teacher. They may refer to attitudes, interpersonal skills, group work, or study skills—or whatever the teacher considers a concomitant attribute of learning. These too should be made explicit on the printout. Some examples of these are found in chapter 9, "Students as Self-Evaluators."

Self-evaluation forms may include narratives only; they may include rating scales that refer to frequency or level of accomplishment. They may include combinations of both. But the essential feature of these forms should be their reflection of the standards and goals—that is, what's important in the student's learning.

Students should engage in such self-evaluation exercises regularly; too often makes the activity dreaded. Too infrequent makes it less important. It should become a normal part of school life—training and educating students to become more tuned into their own learning needs and successes.

In addition to these self-evaluation profiles, students should be encouraged to keep and update portfolios—ongoing records of their work, including copies of their self-evaluations. This cumulative record becomes the basis for the summative evaluation at the end of the year, or semester.

The summative evaluation is done in a student-teacher conference, where the students' work in the portfolio is presented and discussed and a final grade is determined with the student in consultation with the teacher. The student's role in this determination is an important feature of his and her growing understanding of the nature and quality of the work done.

This is a "soft" response to working within the constraints of the school or district requirements vis-à-vis evaluation. Nothing about these strategies will imperil a teacher or cause administrative alarm.

b. A More Radical Idea

This takes a giant step toward student self-evaluation. It begins with the strategies articulated above. Students participate in ongoing and continued self-evaluation throughout the year or the term and accumulate their work and their self-assessments in their portfolios.

The summative evaluation is now given over to the student. A "clone" of a final report card is duplicated, and students are given the task of making their own summative evaluation, in a letter or a number (the system prescribed by the school or district). These summative evaluations are discussed, post hoc, with the teacher in a final conference, and unless there is a major discrepancy, the student's assessment should be allowed to stand.

Where there are minor discrepancies between the student's assessment and the teacher's view, these should be discussed, in the absence of reproach, or guilt-invoking, but rather facilitatively and with questions that call for further student reflection on his or her work. When the discrepancy is of major concern, the teacher has a choice. Should the teacher confront the student with examples of why they disagree on the grade? Should she or he allow the grade to stand, even though the teacher does not believe it is a fair assessment? Should the teacher "pick up the ball" and tell the student that he or she is in error? Should the teacher ask for documentation that supports the student's grade from his or her perspective?

Much will depend on the teacher's assessment of the student's needs, values, and concerns. As in life, there is no right answer; there is only what the teacher believes is right decision at that time. Of course, much will be revealed about the student who chooses to ignore the evidence and give himself or herself a better grade. And that is surely an observation that is worth noting.

While this may sound radical and, to some, preposterous, those teachers who have used this approach find that, by and large, most students are honest and more introspective when given the chance to make their self-assessments.

In fact, teachers who attempt this more radical approach may be pleasantly surprised.

END NOTE

This chapter has presented two ideas for teachers who are constrained by administrative fiat to issue letter or number grades that reflect students' learning in a course, subject, or grade. Doubtless, teachers who see the necessity of evaluation systems that support and encourage student learning, instead of ranking them, will have ideas of their own. The ways and means are not as important as the criteria. That is, any system that provides diagnostic feedback to learners, supports them in their efforts to improve, and does not crush their spirits will work.

The system that a teacher originates may be considered a "beta" test—and, once used, should provide that teacher with the kind of feedback that he or she can use to improve the schema—in other words, a flexible tool that may change with new information and new insights into the process.

Involving students in the process has multiple benefits, and it is hoped that these few pages will lead not only to improved student awareness of self as learners but will provide teachers with deeper insights into the nature of student learning.

Chapter 12

Postscript

A Personal Odyssey

To prepare for this textbook on evaluation practices, I read and reread some of the major tomes about evaluation that have graced the shelves of the library for the last thirty or more years, as well as many of the journal articles that dealt with classroom practices as well as administrative dictates. It was a humbling task—to read what some of the more important thinkers in educational practice had to say about evaluation.

Many of them were condemnations of current practice that emphasized grading and ranking of students. Many pointed to the need for clearer and more helpful diagnostic reports to parents. Many declaimed the use of standardized tests as having little or no value in pointing to students' learning needs and the ways in which teachers might address them. More than a few suggested the many benefits of students' involvement in self-assessment. None went beyond admonitions in giving specific examples of the "how"—that is, the application of good ideas to classroom practice. It is the hope of this author that this book remedies that shortfall.

A PROFESSIONAL JOURNEY

It would be fair to say that when I entered the teaching profession, lo these many moons ago, I had as little notion of the "finer art" of evaluation as a newly hatched chick. There was no course in my teacher education program that addressed evaluation. My university professors were strong on the "should" but weak on the "how." Lecturing was the primary mode of instruction. I came away from thirty-six credits in education as a complete and utter dolt.

My first years as a primary teacher were concentrated efforts on keeping children quiet and teaching them the lessons in the teachers' manuals. Grading was done with district-issued report cards and I had little or no sense of how a grade that I determined, in my infinite wisdom, would help or harm a student in terms of future learning. Let alone how fair or accurate was that assessment. Parent-teacher conferences took up some of the shortfall and through these I began to get a glimpse of the anxiety that parents showed, some more overtly, about their child's academic work.

Visiting other schools on what were called "Professional Days" showed me classrooms and teaching that were as different from mine as a hatchling is different from a full-grown swan. Little by little, through school visits, readings, and graduate coursework, I began to understand more about teaching and learning and how I might introduce more child-centered ideas into my classroom. Even so, evaluation as marking and ranking persisted. As traditional teachers come, I was part of the multitudes.

That is, until I began to observe, to really discern what I was doing and became more tuned into the effects. The three reading groups, to which I was wedded, began to become unglued. I could see that in each of the groups there were children at each end who did not fit. No matter how I might try to squeeze them into the Robins or the Bluebirds, some lagged behind and others were constrained from racing ahead. I could see that something needed fixing and badly.

As luck would have it, on another Professional Day, a visitor from a nearby university came to talk to the teachers about Individualized Reading. She was critical of the deeply ingrained practice of reading groups, citing how they failed to deal with each individual in the group—a concern that touched me to the quick. She didn't back down from providing us with specific advice on how to implement such a program in our classrooms. I had been wooed and won.

Once I fell to the call of individualization of instruction in reading, I could not fail to see why it needed to be applied in other subject areas. Thus began a sea change in my conceptualization of what teaching could and should be, and how new methods could and should be applied to ensure that individual learning needs were attended to across the curriculum and how learners could and should benefit from more hands-on work in groups that focused on investigative inquiry.

In a sixth-grade class, with thirty-two students in a suburban elementary school on Long Island, I ventured forth to initiate a student-centered program in which students' choice, self-pacing, group work, project-based learning, and self-evaluation were key elements in my teaching. The more I gave my students permission and encouragement to be self-sustaining, the more they surprised and delighted me with what they could do.

Shifting gears to teacher education at the university did not constrain my beliefs in using methods that were more student-centered and that modeled what I hoped would be the methods that my students would use in their own classrooms—that is, emphasis not only on the what, but on the how. Self-evaluation in all of my teacher education courses was a strong concomitant to all the other methods I used.

I have never looked back.

In this text, I have advocated for change—a change in the ways in which learners are evaluated, and I have given many examples of how this might be done—either as innovations or within the constraints of a traditional classroom. But of course, in the end, it falls to each teacher—for, as in all things that happen in classrooms, it is the teacher who is the key.

Bibliography

Adam, Maureen. 1992. The Responses of Eleventh Graders to Use of Case Method of Instruction in Social Studies. Unpublished Master's thesis, Faculty of Education, Simon Fraser University, Burnaby, BC.

Adam, Maureen, Chambers, Rich, Fukui, Steve, Gluska, Joe and Wassermann, Selma. 1991. *Evaluation Materials for the Graduate Program*. Victoria, BC: B.C. Ministry of Education.

Aikens, Wilford M. 1948. *The Story of the Eight-Year Study*. New York: Harper & Brothers.

Bernard, Renee and Boothby, Lauren. 2019. "Vancouver Schools Test New Report Cards, Scrapping Letter Grades for Elementary Students." https:www.citynews1130.com/2019/02/15/Vancouver-schools-test.

Bickerton, Laura, Chambers, Rich, Dart, George, Fukui, Steve, Gluska, Joe, McNeill, Brenda, Odermatt, Paul and Wassermann, Selma. 1991. *Cases for Teaching in the Secondary School*. Coquitlam, BC: Caseworks.

Bok, Derek. 2006. *Our Underachieving Colleges*. Princeton, NJ: Princeton University Press.

Bowles, Samuel and Gintis, Herbert. 1976. *Schooling in Capitalist America: Educational Reform and the Contradictions of Economic Life*. New York: Basic Books.

British Columbia Ministry of Education. 1990. *The Graduation Program*. Victoria, B.C.

Carkhuff, Robert. 1969. *Helping and Human Relations*, Vol. 1. New York: Holt, Rinehart & Winston.

Combs, Arthur W. 1979. *Myths in Education*. Boston: Allyn & Bacon.

Cremin, Lawrence A. 1961. *The Transformation of the School*. New York: Alfred Knopf.

Cromwell, Sharon. 2015. "Student-Led Conferences: A Growing Trend." *Education World*. https://www.educationworld.com.

Cuban, Larry. 1990. "Reforming Again, Again, and Again." *Educational Researcher*, Vol. 19, No. 1, pp. 3–13.

Cuban, Larry. 2008. *Frogs into Princes*. New York: Teachers College Press.
Cuban, Larry. 2013. *Inside the Black Box of Classroom Practice*. Cambridge, MA: Harvard University Press.
Cuban, Larry and Tyack, David. 1997. *Tinkering Toward Utopia*. Cambridge, MA: Harvard University Press.
Downes, Olin. 1928. New York Times Review. In Slonimsky, 1965. *Lexicon of Musical Invective*. Washington, DC: Coleman-Ross Co.
Dubal, David. 2004. *Evenings with Horowitz*. New York: Amadeus.
Durm, Mark. 1993. "An A Is Not an A Is Not an A: A History of Grading." *The Educational Forum*, Vol. 57, pp. 294–298.
Finkelstein, Isadore E. 1913. "The Marking System in Theory and Practice." *Educational Psychology Monographs*, p. 10.
French, Marilyn. 1985. *Beyond Power*. New York: Summit Books.
Gleick, James. 1999. *Faster*. New York: Vintage Books.
Good, Jere E. and Brophy, Thomas. 1974. *Teacher-Student Relationships: Causes and Consequences*. London: Holt, Rinehart and Winston.
Gould, Stephen Jay. 1981. *The Mismeasure of Man*. New York: Norton.
Hoffman, Banesh. 1964. *The Tyranny of Testing*. New York: Collier.
Jussim, L. and Harber, K. D. 2005. "Teacher Expectations and Self-Fulfilling Prophecies: Knows and Unknowns Resolved and Unresolved Controversies." *Personality and Social Psychology Review*, Vol. 9, No. 2, pp. 131–155.
Juster, Norton. 1961. *The Phantom Tollbooth*. New York: Random House.
Kirschenbaum, Howard, Napier, Rodney and Simon, Sidney. 1971. *Wad-ja-Get? The Grading Game in American Education*. New York: Hart.
Kohn, Alfie. 1999. *Punished by Rewards*. Boston: Mariner Books.
Kohn, Alfie. 2012. *Schooling Beyond Measure*. New Hampshire: Heinemann.
MacDonald, Cheryl. 1982. "A Better Way of Reporting." *B. C. Teacher*, Vol. 61, pp. 142–144.
Moustakas, Clark. 1966. *The Authentic Teacher*. Cambridge, MA: Howard Doyle.
Owen, David. 1985. *None of the Above*. Boston: Houghton Mifflin.
Peyser, Herbert 1928. New York Telegram Review. In Slominsky, 1965. *Lexicon of Musical Invective*. Washington, DC. Coleman-Ross Co.
Rogers, Carl. 1961. *On Becoming a Person*. Boston: Houghton Mifflin.
Rosenthal, Robert and Jacobson Lenore. 1992. *Pygmalion in the Classroom: Teacher Expectations and Pupils Intellectual Development*. Bancyfelin, Carmarthen, Wales: Crown House.
Ryan, William. 1981. *Equality*. New York: Pantheon Books.
Slonimsky, Nicolas. 1965. *Lexicon of Musical Invective*. Washington, DC: Coleman-Ross Co.
Spencer, Kyle. 2017. "A New Kind of Classroom: No Grades, No Failing, No Hurry." *New York Times*, August 11, 2017.
Stiggins, Rick 2009. "Assessment FOR Learning in Upper Elementary Grades." *Phi Delta Kappan*, February, Vol. 90, No. 6, pp. 419–421.
Taylor, Kate and Bosman, Julie. 2019. "Felicity Huffman's Guilty Plea Could Bring 4 Months in Jail." *New York Times*, May 13, 2019.

Tyack, David. 1974. *One Best System: A History of American Urban Education.* Cambridge, MA: Harvard University Press.

Tyack, David and Cuban, Larry. 1995. *Tinkering Toward Utopia.* Cambridge, MA: Harvard University Press.

Vancouver School Board. 2018. *Teaching and Learning: Assessment and Reporting.* https://www.vsb.bc.ca/schools/charles-dickens-annex/Teaching and Learning Pages/default.aspx.

Wassermann, Selma. 1990. *Serious Players in the Primary Classroom. Empowering Children Through Active Learning Experiences.* New York: Teachers College Press.

Wassermann, Selma. 1991. "Teaching Strategies: What's Evaluation For?" *Childhood Education*, Winter, pp. 93–98.

Wassesrmann, Selma. 2007. "Dare to Be Different." *Phi Delta Kappan*, January, Vol. 88, No. 5, pp. 384–390.

Wassermann, Selma. 2015. "What is Teaching? Inside the Black Box of What Teachers Do." *Childhood Education*, Vol. 91, No. 2, pp. 83–89.

Wassermann, Selma. 2017. *The Art of Interactive Teaching.* New York: Routledge.

Wassemann, Selma and Eggert, Wallace. 1976. "Profiles of Teaching Competency." *Canadian Journal of Education*, Vol. 1, No. 67, p. 11.

Wassermann, Selma and Eggert, Wallace. 1981. "Profiles of Teaching Competency." *Eric Clearinghouse on Teacher Education*, Spring, 1981.

Wassermann, Selma and Ivany, J. W. George. 1996. *The New Teaching Elementary Science: Who's Afraid of Spiders.* New York: Teachers College Press.

Wilhelms, Fred T. and Diederich, Paul B. 1967. "The Fruits of Freedom." In Wilhelms, Fred, ed. *Evaluation as Feedback and Guide.* Washington, DC: Association for Supervision and Curriculum Development, 1967 Yearbook.

Index

Adam, Maureen, 61, 63, 79, 91
Aikens, Wilford M., 111
attends to ideas of others, 102
attitudes: beliefs and values, 104; personal perspectives of, 103; self-evaluation of, 104–105

beliefs, 6, 10, 13, 18, 64, 91, 104
Bernard, Renee, 108, 116
Beyond Power (French), 7
Bickerton, Laura, 61
Bok, Derek, 13, 16
Boothby, Lauren, 108, 116
Bosman, Julie, 107
Bowles, Samuel, 8
British Columbia, Canada: evaluative feedback in reporting to parents, 114–16; Ministry of Education, 91, 109, 115

Carkhuff, Robert, 70
Chambers, Rich, 91
Charles Dickens Elementary School Annex: evaluative feedback in reporting to parents, 109–12; new reporting schedule, 112; student learning, communicating, 111
checklist, for evaluative feedback, 24–25
classroom discussions, 57–64

collaborative professional partnership, 56–57
Combs, Arthur W., 2
Common Core State Standards, 9
communication of ideas, 100
competence, and marking and grading system, 13
competency-based learning. *See* mastery learning
Cremin, Lawrence A., 8
Cromwell, Sharon, 80
Cuban, Larry, 2, 9–10, 114, 118, 119

Dewey, John, 117
Diederich, Paul B., 13, 16–18, 20–21
Downes, Olin, xiv
Dubal, David, 7
Durm, Mark, 16
Dwight-Englewood School: evaluative feedback in reporting to parents, 108–109

Educational Testing Service, 9
Eggert, Wallace, 117
empathy, 70
evaluation: criteria for, 23–24; definition of, 1–6; as feedback, 19–20; practices, 26; as subversive activity, 119–22

evaluative feedback, 17–22; checklist, 24–25; criteria, identification of, 25; growth and, 23–28; learning goals and evaluation practices, 26; in lieu of grades, obstacles to, 20–22; measurement, 25–26; to parents, 5; in reporting to parents, institutional changes toward using, 107–18; science program, goals for, 27–28; to students, 4–5; written, across the curriculum, 29

feedback. *See* evaluative feedback
Finkelstein, Isadore E., xv, 2, 16
force of habit, 1–3
French, Marilyn, 7–9
Fukui, Steve, 91

Gintis, Herbert, 8
Gleick, James, 12
Gluska, Joe, 91
Gould, Stephen Jay, 16
grading system, 2–3; failings of, 7–16
grammar of schooling, 2, 9–10
group discussion, contributes to facilitation of, 102

Hechinger Report, 113–14
Hoffman, Banesh, 16
house of cards, 10–16
Hunter, Madeline, 109

impediments to good diagnostic judgment, 67–71; advice to teachers, 70–71; impulse to punish by evaluative judgment, taming, 69–70
information: collecting and organizing, 101; extracting and recording, 101–102
institutional changes toward using evaluative feedback in reporting to parents, 107–18; British Columbia, Canada, 114–16; Charles Dickens Elementary School Annex, 109–12; Dwight-Englewood School, 108–109; Little Red Schoolhouse, 112–13; New York City, 113–14; Simon Fraser University, 116–17
intermediate grades: written diagnostic evaluative feedback, 37–43
interpersonal skills: attends to the ideas of others, 102; group discussion, contributes to facilitation of, 102
Ivany, J. W. George, 60

Juster, Norton, 12

Kirschenbaum, Howard, 16
Kohn, Alfie, 16, 55, 64

learning goals, 26
Little Red Schoolhouse: evaluative feedback in reporting to parents, 112–13
love affair with numbers, 11–13

MacDonald, Cheryl, 79, 80
MacKinnon, Archie, 116
marking system, 2–3; failings of, 7–16
mastery learning, 113
Moustakas, Clark, 69

Napier, Rodney, 16
New York City schools: evaluative feedback in reporting to parents, 113–14
No Child Left Behind, 9

obedience, 8
one-on-one tutorial, self-evaluation in, 89–90
Owen, David, 16

parent-student-teacher conferences, 78–81
parent-teacher conferences, 78–81
Pass-Withdraw system, 117
performance, and marking and grading system, 13–14
personal perspectives of attitudes, 103–104
Peyser, Herbert, xiv

The Phantom Tollbooth, 12
portfolio review, 93–94
positive world outlook, 103
praise, 64–65
primary grades: self-evaluation in, 86–87; written diagnostic evaluative feedback, 30–37; written self-evaluation reports in, 87–89
Professional Days, 124
professional journey, 123–25
Profiles of Student Behaviors, 95–104; attitudes, 103–104; intellectual development, 96–99; skills, 100–102
Profiles of Student Competencies, 117

quality of thinking: big ideas, 96–97; fact–assumptions difference, 97; fact–opinion difference, 97; intelligent interpretation of data, 98–99; opinions of others, 97; original, inventive, creative work, 99; support of ideas, 98; thinking as a way of life, embracing, 99; tolerance for contrary data, 98; tolerance for ideas, 97

reflecting in action, 55–57
regular student self-evaluation, as integral part of student learning, 120–21
reliability of marking and grading system, 10–11
reporting to parents, 73–81; institutional changes toward using evaluative feedback in, 107–18; parent-student-teacher conferences, 78–81; parent-teacher conferences, 78–81; written reports, 74–78
research skills: information, collecting and organizing, 101; information, extracting and recording, 101–102
Rogers, Carl, 18
Rooney, George, 110
Ryan, William, 8

science program, goals for, 27–28

secondary school: self-evaluation in, 89–105; Profiles of Student Behaviors, 95–104; student portfolios, 93–94; summative evaluation report, 94–95; Thinking Logs, 91–93; written diagnostic evaluative feedback, 43–52
self-assessment task, 92–93
self-evaluation, 4, 6, 23, 29, 79, 83, 86, 91: open to, 104–105; regular student, as integral part of student learning, 120–21; report, summative, 94–95; skill in, 105; written reports, in primary grades, 87–89
self-evaluators, students as, 83; one-on-one tutorial, 89–90; primary grades, 86–89; secondary school, 89–104; teachers' assessments on profiles, 105
Simon, Sidney, 16
Simon Fraser University: Pass-Withdraw system, 117; Professional Development Program, 116; teacher education program, 116–17
skills: communication of ideas, 100; interpersonal, 102; research, 101–102; in self-evaluation, 105
Slonimsky, Nicolas, xiv
social control, 8
speaking, quality of thinking in, 100
Spencer, Kyle, 113, 114
Stanford-Binet I.Q. test, 9
Stiggins, Rick, 106
student's belief about marking and grading system, 13
summative evaluation, 121; report, 94–95

tablet generation, 37
Taylor, Kate, 107
teachers: advice to, for good diagnostic judgment, 70–71; assessments on profiles, 105
Teaching as a Subversive Activity (Postman and Weingartner), 119
Thinking Logs, 91–93

timing of test, and marking and grading system, 15–16
tolerance for ambiguity, 103
Tyack, David, 2, 8–10, 114, 119

validity of marking and grading system, 10–11
values, 104
Vancouver School Board, 111, 115, 116

Wassermann, Selma, 56, 60, 68, 91, 109–11, 117

Wilhelms, Fred T., 13, 16–18, 20–21
world perspective of attitudes, 104
writing, quality of thinking in, 100
written diagnostic evaluative feedback across the curriculum, 29; intermediate grades, 37–43; primary grades, 30–37; secondary school, 43–52
written reports to parents, 74–78
written self-evaluation reports, in primary grades, 87–89

About the Author

Selma Wassermann is professor emerita in the Faculty of Education at Simon Fraser University, Vancouver, Canada. Her books include *Teaching in the Age of Disinformation: Don't Confuse Me with the Data, My Mind Is Made Up!*, *The Art of Discussion Teaching*, *Teaching for Thinking Today: Theory, Strategies and Activities for the Classroom*, *Serious Players in the Primary Classroom*, *The New Teaching Elementary Science*, *This Teaching Life*, and *The Long Distance Grandmother*.

www.ingramcontent.com/pod-product-compliance
Lightning Source LLC
Chambersburg PA
CBHW020747230426
43665CB00009B/529